ADVANCE PRAISE FOR *LEADING VALIANTLY*

"This book is an amazing compilation of theory, exemplars, and lessons learned wrapped in a foundation of leadership integrity. I am so impressed with the intensity of the information, which automatically drives one into deep and thorough personal reflections. This book is for every leader who wants to be the best leader he or she can be!"

–Rhonda Anderson, DNSc, RN, FAAN, FACHE
Chief Executive Officer
Cardon Children's Medical Center

"Excellent leadership motivates leaders to continually do and be their very best, but valiant leadership is about so much more. Robinson-Walker's 30-year commitment to nursing and nursing leadership is unparalled, and her new book is so wonderful: Read, learn, and enjoy!"

–Roxane Spitzer, PhD, MBA, RN, FAAN
Editor in Chief, *Nurse Leader*, Official Magazine of the
American Organization of Nurse Executives
VP Executive Strategist for Onsomble

"Leading Valiantly in Healthcare *is an important book for today's leaders. Some leadership books you read and then put away. This is a book that can provide guided learning and splendid content for personal reflection beyond the first reading. Thank you, Cathy Robinson-Walker, for giving us a book for our minds, our hearts, and our souls. I accept your invitation to begin to walk this path."*

–Pamela Austin Thompson, MS, RN, CENP, FAAN
CEO, American Organization of Nurse Executives
Senior VP for Nursing, American Hospital Association

"Leading Valiantly in Healthcare *is an artful combination of insight and wisdom, shared in a fashion that will resonate with any contemporary leader. This book offers readers the rare opportunity to engage in personal executive coaching, with a nationally renowned master certified executive coach at their fingertips!"*

–Dana Nicholson Bledsoe
President, Children's and Women's Hospital
Sacred Heart Health System

"If you strive to be a more confident, courageous leader, this thought-provoking book is for you. This book is about becoming the best leader you can be. A leader acts bravely and with integrity to accomplish what needs to be done, no matter how difficult the situation."

–Patricia Lenihan McFarland, MS, RN, FAAN
CEO of Association of California Nurse Leaders, California
Nursing Students' Association, and California Association of Colleges of Nursing

"Robinson-Walker imparts her vast knowledge and experience in leadership development and executive coaching to provide leaders with an innovative, step-by-step approach for leading valiantly: to do what matters most, to make a difference in healthcare—one leader and one organization at a time. Via realistic vignettes and practical exercises, her prescription for leadership well-being is a must-read and a must-do for leaders within healthcare settings."

–Lynda Olender, MA, RN, NEA-BC
Director of Nursing and Patient Care Services
Rockefeller University Hospital

"A great read for all leaders in healthcare today!"

–Judith G. Berg, MS, RN, FACHE
Executive Director
California Institute for Nursing and Health Care

"Leading Valiantly in Healthcare *is a must-read for all leaders who wish to embrace the true essence of why they became leaders in the first place. Robinson-Walker's vast experience with executive coaching lifts up a whole other level of leadership practice that previously has gone unacknowledged. This book is destined to become a leadership classic."*

–Elaine L. Cohen, EdD, RN, FAAN
Chief, Nursing Quality Improvement
Support Services/Magnet Director
James A. Haley Veterans' Hospital

"Nurse leaders need Robinson-Walker's book. I particularly appreciated her Cycle of Valor and how to use it in real-life situations. At the end of the day, using her book as a reference, one can self-reflect and use the 'guideposts' to develop strategies to become better leaders."

–KT Waxman, DNP, MBA, RN, CNL, CENP
Assistant Professor
Director, Doctor of Nursing Practice Program
University of San Francisco

"Robinson-Walker has written a superb and unique leadership book— different from any other I have read. We see how wonderfully fallible we all are, and Robinson-Walker's map for understanding how to lead valiantly paves a path forward. Her message is both clear and inspirational; if leaders follow the call to lead with valor, both people and organizations will be transformed."

–Kathleen Stinnett, MCC
Founder of Future Launch and author of
The Extraordinary Coach: How the Best Leaders Help Others Grow

"More leadership thinking needs to incorporate the character traits of courage and valor with the strategy that comes with good thinking and the emotional intelligence skills that have a lasting impact. We need to thank Robinson-Walker for this book."

–John P. Schuster
Executive Coach
Author of *Answering Your Call* and
The Power of Your Past: The Art of Recalling, Reclaiming and Recasting

"Brilliantly conceived and deftly articulated, this book provides exquisitely sound and practical tools for those who chose to be leaders in their personal and professional lives! It is simply elegant and a profoundly rich read, an essential guide for all leaders who espouse empowerment and shared leadership in their organizations."

–Jayne Felgen, MPA, RN
President Emeritus
Creative Health Care Management

"Everyone involved in leadership—as well as aspiring leaders—will gain some valuable insights from this book that can be applied to leadership across the continuum and valor sustainability."

–Franklin (Frank) A. Shaffer, EdD, RN, FAAN
Chief Executive Officer, CGFNS International

"Leading Valiantly is a unique contribution to healthcare leadership. The insights and practices you'll learn are certain to provide a way forward for you and your team."

–Diane Brennan, MBA, FACMPE, MCC
Master Certified Coach, Brennan Associates
Past President, International Coach Federation

"In her newest contribution to healthcare leadership, Robinson-Walker demonstrates the wisdom that comes from combining passion with a lifetime commitment to healthcare leadership. Her many experiences and examples are laced with insight that emerge from combining intelligence of the mind with the warmth of a compassionate heart. This book will transform the field."

–JoEllen Koerner, PhD, RN
VP Learning Strategies
InteractiveThink.com

"As valiant leaders, we must lead the charge and be the change we want to see across today's complex healthcare continuum. Leading Valiantly in Healthcare offers inspiration for all with the courage, integrity and compassion to lead these individuals during challenging times."

–Donna L. Kistler, MS, RN
Director, Patient Care Services
Stanford Hospital and Clinics

"Leading Valiantly in Healthcare is the next generation of leadership self-help. The book is an intriguing and enticing read, as Robinson-Walker stretches our imagination and understanding of leadership. This is a must-read for leaders who must now draw on character, self-control, integrity and valor to lead in a transformed healthcare system."

–BJ Bartleson, MS, RN, NEA-BC
Vice President, Nursing & Clinical Services
California Hospital Association

"This book is a pragmatic and personal guide to courageous, forthright leadership in healthcare. During sweeping, systemic change, patients require leaders who are present to themselves, able to make courageous choices, and willing to take a stand. Robinson-Walker shows how to become the most grounded and conscious leaders we can be."

–Doug Silsbee, PCC
Leadership Coach, Speaker, and
Author, Presence-Based Coaching

"This book is for anyone who wants to lead more consciously with an open mind and an open heart in the complex, high-stakes environment of healthcare. Robinson-Walker valiantly offers a set of tools to help us bring with purpose and clarity our best selves to our leadership roles each day."

–Susan M. Coe, MBA
Director, Employee & Labor Relations
University of Maryland Medical System

"Robinson-Walker combines her keen wisdom, deep appreciation, and endearing compassion as she eloquently weaves stories of real-life challenges faced by today's healthcare leaders. She fully embraces the necessity of self-care as healthcare leaders navigate the tightrope of their profession with adequate work/life balance."

–Kim Richards, RN, NC-BC
President, Kim Richards and Associates, Inc.
President, Self-Care Academy, LLC

To Lee Anne, a valiant leader.

From, Debra Jeffs

2014

LEADING
Valiantly
IN HEALTHCARE

FOUR STEPS TO SUSTAINABLE SUCCESS

CATHERINE ROBINSON-WALKER, MBA, MCC

Sigma Theta Tau International
Honor Society of Nursing®

The Honor Society of Nursing, Sigma Theta Tau International (STTI) is a nonprofit organization whose mission is to support the learning, knowledge, and professional development of nurses committed to making a difference in health worldwide. Founded in 1922, STTI has 130,000 members in 86 countries. Members include practicing nurses, instructors, researchers, policymakers, entrepreneurs, and others. STTI's 487 chapters are located at 663 institutions of higher education throughout Australia, Botswana, Brazil, Canada, Colombia, Ghana, Hong Kong, Japan, Kenya, Malawi, Mexico, the Netherlands, Pakistan, Portugal, Singapore, South Africa, South Korea, Swaziland, Sweden, Taiwan, Tanzania, United Kingdom, United States, and Wales. More information about STTI can be found online at www.nursingsociety.org.

Sigma Theta Tau International
550 West North Street
Indianapolis, IN, USA 46202

To order additional books, buy in bulk, or order for corporate use, contact Nursing Knowledge International at 888.NKI.4YOU (888.654.4968/US and Canada) or +1.317.634.8171 (outside US and Canada).

To request a review copy for course adoption, e-mail solutions@nursingknowledge.org or call 888. NKI.4YOU (888.654.4968/US and Canada) or +1.317.634.8171 (outside US and Canada).

To request author information, or for speaker or other media requests, contact Marketing, Honor Society of Nursing, Sigma Theta Tau International at 888.634.7575 (US and Canada) or +1.317.634.8171 (outside US and Canada).

ISBN: 9781937554835
EPUB ISBN: 9781937554842
PDF ISBN: 9781937554859
MOBI ISBN: 9781937554866

Library of Congress Cataloging-in-Publication Data

Robinson-Walker, Catherine, 1946-
  Leading valiantly in healthcare : four steps to sustainable success / Catherine Robinson-Walker.
    p. ; cm.
  ISBN 978-1-937554-83-5 (alk. paper) -- ISBN 978-1-937554-84-2 (epub) -- ISBN 978-1-937554-85-9 (PDF) -- ISBN 978-1-937554-86-6 (MOBI)
    I. Sigma Theta Tau International. II. Title.
    [DNLM: 1. Leadership. 2. Professional Competence. 3. Administrative Personnel. 4. Delivery of Health Care. 5. Health Services Administration. W 21]
    RA971.35
    362.1068'3--dc23
                        2013013434

First Printing, 2013

Publisher: Renee Wilmeth
Acquisitions Editor: Emily Hatch
Editorial Coordinator: Paula Jeffers
Copy Editor: Erin Geile
Cover Designer: Pamela Frazier
Interior Design/Page Layout: Rebecca Batchelor

Principal Book Editor: Carla Hall
Consulting Editor: Katherine J. Armstrong
Development and Project Editor: Jennifer Lynn
Proofreaders: Erin Geile and Jane Palmer
Indexer: Johnna Van Hoose Dinse

DEDICATION

To our healers, in their many forms.

ACKNOWLEDGMENTS

Tempted as I am to thank the many people who have gifted me with their wisdom over the years, there is no way that I can adequately recognize each of these individuals in this short piece. So, my focus here is on those who have supported me specifically during the creation of *Leading Valiantly in Healthcare*.

I am eternally grateful for the backing and reinforcement I have received from family and friends throughout this journey; indeed, the journey would not have been possible without them. My husband, Tim, has shown me qualities of love and unending patience that tell me yet again how fortunate I am to have him as my life partner. Dear friends Kate Crawford, Maya Mahrer, Kathleen Aw, Lynn Schoener, Kay Starkweather, Vera Goupille, and Peggy Shultz have all offered me soul-sustaining solace and encouragement along the way.

Dr. Angeles Arrien's coaching and mentoring in the "Should I do this?" years were deeply nurturing. In a similar vein, Galen Friend's counsel was also a great gift. In addition, there are a number of colleagues whose insights, ideas, and resources influenced me in the early years of this book. Among them are Donna Wright, Pam Thompson, Marla Weston, Nancy Rollins Gantz, Nancy Valentine, Kathy Vestal, Elizabeth Doty, and John Schuster. The Bay Area coaching colleagues with whom I met regularly during the formative years of this book contributed valuable perspectives, too: Cheryl Mann, Grace Boda, and Charlotte Toothman. An invitation from the Consultants Consortium to facilitate their retreat using these principles came at precisely the right time, and the participants' enthusiastic embrace of their own Leadership Valor was more than heartening.

I will always be thankful for the rich and textured understanding of coaching that prepared me for my work as an executive coach and, by extension, for writing this book. It is impossible to overstate the positive impact of my many years of association with The Hudson Institute of Coaching, specifically Drs. Pamela McLean and Frederick Hudson, and my splendid colleagues on the Hudson Institute's Leadership Team. My work with other luminaries in the coaching world has deepened my appreciation and practice of the important subtleties of executive coaching, too: Dr. Faith Fuller and Marita Fridjhon of The Center for Right Relationship, Inc., Doug Silsbee of Presence-Based Leadership Development, and Dr. Dorothy Siminovitch, recognized pioneer of "Gestalt Coaching," to name a few.

As the book took form, I had the good fortune of participating in and being nurtured by the Berrett-Koehler author community. That led me to the door of Mark Levy who so deftly guided me through the thicket of finding just the right label to convey the beauty I so frequently witness in exceptional healthcare leaders.

Roxane Spitzer, Rhonda Anderson, Kathleen Stinnett, and Julie Hess kindly offered their time and feedback after my ideas coalesced and I started writing. My team of Leadership Studio support staff, including Anna Maria Granato, Dee Renfro, and Connie Glover, earn my gratitude every day, but especially during the months of preparing this manuscript. I also greatly appreciate the focus and care consistently offered by Renee Wilmeth, Emily Hatch, Carla Hall, and the entire team at Sigma Theta Tau International.

It is difficult to find the words to express my everlasting gratitude for my fearless freelance editor, Katherine Armstrong. Her guidance for more than 2 years helped me find "the" book among several possibilities and weather numerous difficult turns in the book-writing road. Her support was not just occasional; it was daily, consistent, and always positive. Substantive, learned, and always gracious support of a different kind was offered by Dr. Elaine Cohen, who was willing and eager to read every word of the book as I created it. Our many conversations were deliciously rich, informative, and influential as I prepared the final manuscript.

Lastly, I recognize those who have inspired me every step of the way. None of these words would be on these pages were it not for my clients, the organizations, teams, and individual leaders who have asked me to work with them during my many years in this field. The quality of their leadership has profoundly affected me and created the impetus for each idea and exercise in this book. My gratitude to them knows no bounds.

About the Author

 **Catherine Robinson-Walker, MBA, MCC,** specializes in leadership development and executive coaching in healthcare. Currently president of The Leadership Studio®, Robinson-Walker has 25 years of executive leadership experience in complex health organizations, national commissions, and academic consortia. She has served physician and nurse leaders, chief executives, management teams, and other senior healthcare staff as a master certified executive coach, strategic consultant, team facilitator, keynote and workshop speaker, and author. She works for national, regional, and local organizations.

Robinson-Walker's first book, *Women and Leadership in Health Care: The Journey to Authenticity and Power* (1999), is a Jossey-Bass health series bestseller. She is the author of numerous continuing education courses and articles, including "The Coaching Forum," a featured column published in *Nurse Leader*, the official journal of the American Organization of Nurse Executives/American Hospital Association.

For 18 years, Robinson-Walker was the founding executive director of the Network for Healthcare Management, a multinational, 15-university consortium of graduate programs in health management, including the University of California Berkeley, the Kellogg School at Northwestern University, and the Wharton School at the University of Pennsylvania. In addition, she has held executive director roles with the Chicago-based Joint Commission and the California Health Collaborative.

Robinson-Walker became an ICF Master Certified Coach in 2005. She has served as a member of the Leadership Team of the renowned Hudson Institute of Coaching since 2001. She is also one of a small number of executive coaches for the National Center for Healthcare Leadership.

Working with nurse leaders has been a special focus for Robinson-Walker since 1982. Since then, she has co-created numerous leadership programs and resources for nurses, including:

❖ **The Network Institute for Patient Care Executives** (also known as The Western Network Institute for Nursing Executives, at the University of California Berkeley)

❖ The inaugural leadership program to launch the **Florence Nightingale Museum of Nursing** building campaign (London)

❖ **The Center for Nursing Leadership Program,** developed in collaboration with the American Organization of Nurse Executives

❖ **The Executive Coaching Resource Center,** an online coaching resource center for members of the American Organization of Nurse Executives

❖ **The Executive Coaching Service,** sponsored and funded by the National Council of State Boards of Nursing (United States)

Robinson-Walker has received considerable recognition throughout her career, including being named "Woman of the Year" by Women Healthcare Executives of Northern California/American College of Healthcare Executives and "Friend of Nursing" by the Association of California Nurse Leaders.

Robinson-Walker has worked in multiple capacities with leaders and teams from a variety of healthcare organizations, such as the American Nurses Association, SSM Health Care, CHOC Children's Hospital of Orange County, the National Council of State Boards of Nursing, John Muir Health, the American Organization of Nurse Executives, the National Cancer Institute, Sutter Health, the Association of California Nurse Leaders, and The Permanente Medical Group.

Through The Leadership Studio, Robinson-Walker teaches, coaches, consults, and speaks on leadership development in the healthcare industry. She lives in Oakland, California.

For more information, please visit Catherine Robinson-Walker's website or email her:

www.leadershipstudio.com
cathy@leadershipstudio.com

TABLE OF CONTENTS

TABLE OF CONTENTS

PREFACE

Providing high-quality healthcare day in and day out is a calling of the soul. But it takes much more than just a "calling" to actually fulfill a critical social need, a vital community promise, and a compelling personal imperative. It takes exceptional skill, dedication, and perseverance. It takes courage, fortitude, and commitment. It takes what many healthcare leaders possess right now, today: It takes the ability to lead valiantly.

The spirit and origins of this book rest with healthcare leaders with just these qualities. This book began with them, and it is inspired by them. These are the leaders with whom I have had the privilege of working for 3 decades. These are leaders who show up fully to meet the ever-increasing challenges of doing more with less and providing more for more, while envisioning and implementing the structural sea changes that these times require.

It is their courageous work that has informed and motivated this book. The reflections, practices, exercises, and wisdom contained in these pages are all derived from my experience of these leaders as bold and highly skilled professionals. These are the leaders who inspire me at every turn; these are the leaders who demonstrate what I call "Leadership Valor."

My years of working with these individuals started with a long engagement as the chief executive of a 15-university consortium devoted to leadership development in healthcare. During those years based at the University of California at Berkeley and the Public Health Institute, I had the chance to work with distinguished professors from all over the United States and Canada as we partnered with professional associations and many of North America's largest healthcare systems. Our charge was to create and implement, with healthcare leaders, the leadership development support they needed and wanted, but were not able to find in any single provider of executive education. From there, I went to the Joint Commission as a senior executive, once again working with distinguished universities and leaders of the major systems in the country.

In 1999, I published a health-series bestseller called *Women and Leadership in Health Care: The Journey to Authenticity and Power* (Jossey-Bass). This book was my first opportunity to give back—to reflect the courageous journeys I was witnessing in these fruitful and inspiring partnerships. In 2000, while still focusing on my work in leadership development, I trained to become an executive coach. Adding that capacity to my long experience with healthcare's stewards deepened my ability to partner with them as both guide of and witness to their growth. In 2005, I earned the distinction of Master Certified Coach, attesting to more than 2,000 paid professional hours as an executive coach, and I have been recertified twice since then. Since 2006 I have served as the featured coaching columnist for *Nurse Leader*, the official publication of the American Organization of Nurse Executives.

The privilege of these experiences gives me a unique vantage point from which to see and analyze frequent patterns that occur on the journey to leadership excellence. I have also had the chance to observe more than just these patterns: I have seen the *essence* of this kind of leadership. From so many perspectives ranging from top-tier, systemwide engagements, to work with leadership teams and their managers, to one-on-one coaching with individual leaders, I have witnessed significant triumphs and show-stopping challenges. I have noticed what leaders do when they are at their best—when they embrace both elegant technical execution and masterful strategies of personal effectiveness. I have also seen the frustrations and barriers that get in the way when they can and want to succeed, but something happens and they "go off the rails."

In my various roles, I have partnered many times with leaders to determine what helps them succeed and consistently be at their best. We have also looked at what has gotten in their way and how it is that they—and only they—are able to bring themselves back to being the leaders they can and want to be.

This book draws on this privileged history and is designed to offer you at least these four benefits:

1. A reflection of who you can be and often are: a courageous, integrity-filled, and valiant steward of our system of care

2. A series of concrete steps and practices that will allow you to claim your own version of Leadership Valor and sustain it with efficacy, personal satisfaction, and solace

3. A way of thinking about how you engage as a leader: a way that builds on the strengths you already possess, and a way that is both feasible and easy to remember

4. Hope, access to, and greater ease with your sense of self, and the leadership assets that are already within you

In this book, I suggest that the question is not, "How can you be a perfect leader?" Nor is it, "How can you be at your best all the time?" Instead, the question is:

> "How can you be at your best—how can you be a truly valiant leader—more and more of the time?"

This is a state that is achievable and sustainable, and this is the question that *Leading Valiantly in Healthcare* answers.

FOREWORD

Much has been written on the topic of healthcare leadership over the past few decades. Yet very little of it addresses the very personal aspects of leadership that affect individual character, role, and behavior and their relationship to personal choice and their place in the larger life journey. Perhaps much of the crisis in leadership relates to the few resources available to leaders to assist them in finding this point of balance between the demands of the role and the personal risks and challenges that influence how well leadership is experienced and expressed.

One frequently hears of generalized reticence on the part of professionals to assume the mantle of leadership. What they have observed jaundices their perception of it and inures them of any interest in pursuing a leadership role. Indeed, the frequent inappropriate or inadequate expression of leadership on so many levels and in so many places creates a general impression of negativity. Those who would otherwise become excellent leaders are both turned off and turned away—precisely at a time when we hunger for effective and meaningful leadership.

The concept of Leadership Valor is an intriguing one. It assumes engagement of an internal compass that connects one's leadership capacity with a sense of self, a clarity of purpose, and the comprehension of one's own meaning. Valor suggests that certain challenges and conflicts in one's personal life journey have been confronted, sorted, and clarified. This does not necessarily mean that such issues have been resolved. Instead, what is implied is a level of willingness to both embrace and engage the uniquely personal yet fundamentally universal contest between comfort and conflict, courage and complacency, and confidence and fear.

Valor also suggests a primordial willingness to meet the challenges of the moment on the field of life as an inexorable and normal part of the leader's life journey. This elemental willingness is often visualized in the personal capacity to aspire beyond the present and to place individual challenge in the context of a larger landscape, harnessing personal energy for a purpose greater than the moment. It is often expressed in the language of "making a difference," "having an impact," or even "changing the world." At the same time, there is a delicacy to valor that calls each of us to caution. We can visualize success, and we can also imagine working against insurmountable odds only to be overcome by defeat.

While valor is a capacity, its expression in leadership is a learned skill. It calls for the leader to develop a level of self-awareness, the capacity to trust the intuitive, refine it, and fine-tune it so that it can become an effective tool in the quiver of leadership competencies. In this arena, the book becomes a critical gift for the learning leader. Through the lens of valor, the reader is able to connect with the premises of valor and through intentional, informed, and paced development, refine that awareness into both a personal capacity and a leadership skill.

The critical skills of a valiant leader can often be recognized in the bearing and expression of the leader. It is often easier to see valor than it is to define it. Valor in the leader is often an expression of the leader's character, fortitude, grace, vulnerability, openness, and honesty. The valiant leader expresses the role from a place that is centered and clear. Present is the serenity and personal calm in the face of an issue's vagaries and intensity in a way that allows the valiant leader to see past the superficial in a problem or challenge, quickly grasp its core, and translate it for others.

At the same time, valor also suggests a continuing commitment
to the persistence and fortitude necessary to carry one past the
momentary, the incidental, the event. The valiant leader is able to
create a contextual framework for life experiences. It is a sort of
scaffolding which serves as the larger architecture within which the
individual designs and constructs life and leadership experiences
so they can unfold with discipline, character, and understanding.
The valiant leader further understands that values broaden and
deepen with learning, exposure, and experience. Valor, for all of its
strengths, demands fluidity so that the foundations of principle
can be nourished with the waters of discovery, insight, and an ever-
deepening discernment. Experience uninformed by learning is no
better than learning undisciplined by experience.

Finally, I think it's important to acknowledge the emphasis in this
wonderful book exemplifying leadership valor: the essential role of
character and courage. Indeed, the essence of both weave through
this text in a subtle but insistent mosaic that suggests to the reader
that valor is for naught if there is a failure to act with courage.
While being valiant is certainly the heartbeat of valor, action is its
evidence. Valor must be demonstrated to have value and not just
expressed at times and in places where it is safe to do so. The real
tests of valor are often witnessed in places where truth has been
sacrificed, errors have occurred, ethics have been ignored, leadership
has failed in its obligations, leaders have hurt others, systems have
lost their way, and missions have been sacrificed. In these circumstances, integrity coalesces with valor. In that moment, the leader
acts with insight and obligation, firmly and with frankness, in a way
that right-sets individual and organizational disequilibrium. It is
here where the individual bears witness to the personal life-work
of valor, demonstrated in its products; the capacity to bring light to

darkness, find right in error, and make good out of wrong, doing so with courage and confidence.

This book provides a wonderful set of insights and tools that best articulates the conceptual, contextual, and functional foundations of valor in its clearest terms. Robinson-Walker has worked diligently and successfully in identifying and enumerating the developmental processes, characteristics, and elements associated with valiant leadership and the critical and often difficult elements that best evidence its foundations. By breaking down its parts, the chapters place valor in context. Through use of a wide variety of real-time scenarios, the book articulates the specific components and characteristics of valor in a way that best evidences its substance and value. However, with all of this book's wisdom, exemplars, and demonstrations of valor, the work of developing personal integrity and courage requires personal insight and effort. In using the wisdom and tools embedded throughout this book, the reader can obtain essential insights that inform the journey to valor and courage. And yet the personal work must still be done. With honesty, openness, willingness, and an intentional level of vulnerability, the use of the insights and tools contained in *Leading Valiantly in Healthcare* can better inform the journey to the integrity of good leadership and the valor that is its best demonstration.

–Tim Porter-O'Grady

INTRODUCTION: WITNESSING LEADERSHIP VALOR

*It's evening. You are getting ready for bed, and you know
you will sleep well tonight. As you think about the day you
spent at work, you feel peaceful. You feel especially good about
the sound decisions you made and the times when you acted
bravely and with full integrity. You feel deeply fulfilled as
you recall those moments when you related well with your
colleagues, were most able to be who you are, and accomplished exactly what needed to be done.*

How often have you experienced this kind of contentment in your
work as a leader? Whether your answer is rarely, sometimes, or
many times, *Leading Valiantly in Healthcare* is about how you can
enjoy this heartfelt sense of leadership satisfaction more often.

I offer this book with the hope and intention that what's here
will equip and inspire you to lead in ways that are uniquely yours,
uniquely effective, and uniquely sustainable. Whether you are a
senior leader in a large health system, a nurse executive or nurse
manager in a hospital or on a unit, or a leader in any other institution that is concerned with communities and their health, I wrote
this book for you.

The wisdom contained herein comes from leaders just like you. In
my 30 years of working in healthcare, I have had the privilege of
partnering with more than 3,000 executives, managers, and clinicians at all levels of the system, all around the United States. I have
engaged with groups ranging in size from hundreds, to gatherings

of 40 to 50, to smaller teams, to pairs of just two people. I have also worked with many individual executives.

What these leaders—predominantly nurses, physicians, professional administrators, and managers—have in common is that they have very tough jobs, often directing, influencing, or making decisions that literally affect people's lives. If you are one of these professionals, you know what I mean. You may be required to attend to multiple patient and managerial needs simultaneously. You may also need to address complex problems involving care units, hospitals, or whole systems with hundreds of millions of dollars and the experience of many patients, their families, and thousands of healthcare workers at stake.

In my work, I have collaborated with leaders like you as a master certified executive coach, leadership development guide, consultant, and executive director of healthcare ventures. In these capacities I have had the privilege of witnessing how leaders like you grapple with their challenges, how they grow and learn, and how they evolve to meet the demands of their roles. In other words, I have seen leaders like you when they are able to do their best work. And, significantly, I also have seen them when they go off the rails.

LEADERSHIP VALOR

From studying how these exemplary—and entirely human— leaders act, I have devised a leadership model that I call the *Cycle of Leadership Valor*. This Cycle frames, distills, and reflects what these inspired leaders do when they are at their best. I see how they increase their personal capacity to achieve better and better results. I see what they put in place so they can lead this way more reliably.

When they do go off the rails, I see the steps they take to self-correct. I see how they return to their core and how they regain access to the vision, skill, and behavior that characterize them when they are at their best.

The word I use to describe this type of leadership is "valor." While we normally think of valor as meaning brave and courageous, I am expanding its definition to include other capacities that these leaders demonstrate when they are fully effective and fully human at the same time. Yes, they show valor in the traditional sense of the word, but they also display qualities that are deeper and richer. These leaders are:

❖ Grounded   ❖ Clear

❖ Open   ❖ Flexible

❖ Confident   ❖ Purposeful

❖ Inspired

These are very powerful men and women.

Theirs is a form of leadership that buoys work teams, peers, and other followers. Theirs is leadership that is sustainable because it is both human and humane. Theirs is leadership that inspires and motivates. Theirs is leadership that succeeds, in part, because it is perfectly imperfect. Theirs is what I call Leadership Valor.

Leadership Valor is at once a state of being, a process of doing, and a leadership "destination" or outcome. It is a state we can find in ourselves and also a state we can aspire to and practice, more and more of the time.

Eventually you will find that the conscious choice of leading in this way and the deliberate process of "getting there" will fade away as you practice. Once you have developed and integrated your own brand of Leadership Valor into your way of leading, it will always be there for you to draw on when new challenges arise.

"Leadership Valor is at once a state of being, a process of doing, and a leadership 'destination' or outcome."

INTEGRITY AND BRAVERY

Stemming from integrity, Leadership Valor invites congruence between who you truly are and what you are working toward every day so that you can experience more success, greater resilience, less stress, and better results.

Leadership Valor is first and foremost a way for you to see and manage yourself. It is a way of being brave enough to:

❖ Consider the options rather than habitually responding to demanding situations or opportunities

❖ Tune into yourself when your results are not what you want or when the stakes are high

❖ Be ready to fully engage even when you are uncertain about next steps

❖ Make and implement conscious, sometimes difficult, choices

❖ Adjust course as needed, even when doing so is problematic

❖ Deliberately integrate what you are learning along the way

WHY LEADERSHIP VALOR? WHY NOW?

Many barriers stand in the way of leading valiantly in healthcare today. We all experience constant and unrelenting pressures on our time and attention. Keeping up with the demands of providing quality patient care is, by itself, both an inspired calling and a daily challenge. When coupled with the shifting landscape in payment and the realities of population-based care, these pressures can pull us in many directions at once. In this situation, it can be tempting to depend on routine thinking and tried-and-true solutions. While these means of leading are sometimes sufficient, relying on them exclusively will stunt our growth and render both our solutions and our presence less effective than either could be.

Society's ever-expanding need for healthcare requires that each of us, as leaders, operates with our full range of skill and focus. Our environment also demands that we are strong and confident as we work to achieve better outcomes for less cost. Leaders who excel in this milieu embrace their experience and their humanity in ways that accelerate rather than hinder the process of providing excellent healthcare.

I offer this book to equip you to do just this—that is, to bring forth the best in yourself as you craft solutions to today's healthcare challenges.

TAPPING INTO LEADERSHIP VALOR, MORE AND MORE OF THE TIME

This book draws on a number of timeless and universal themes. One of them is "mastery." To *master* Leadership Valor is to embrace and accept the state of leading courageously more frequently rather than trying to achieve the largely unattainable goal of leading perfectly 100% of the time.

As in other traditions of mastery, to lead valiantly is to understand that practice is essential. All of us must practice to develop and become successful with our own unique way of leading. Practice does not have to be hard work, but it does require your willingness to try new behaviors, make different choices, and learn what works and what doesn't. Practice does not guarantee a challenge-free leadership life, no matter how skilled you are or how much time you dedicate to it. But when challenges present themselves, practice will permit you to draw on the wisdom and learning you cultivate on your way to leading valiantly.

"Practice will permit you to draw on the wisdom and learning you cultivate on your way to leading valiantly."

In addition to practice, these other aspects of leading with valor are key to making it work for you:

- ❖ **Readiness,** an indication of how prepared you are to move ahead. "Moving ahead" may mean taking a tough stand even when it's difficult, choosing to reflect on how you are leading, considering whether you are operating from a position of full-bodied integrity, or contemplating whether a "Leadership Seduction" is influencing you.

- ❖ **Resistance,** a natural human state that can provide you with valuable information about your own leadership and how you may want (or need) to adjust it.

- ❖ **Reflection,** long known as a best practice in leadership, and which is vital to developing Leadership Valor.

- ❖ **Bravery,** a key ingredient in leading in any fashion in today's world.

- ❖ **Acceptance of imperfection,** your willingness not to be an expert in all matters and not to always have all the answers.

THE CYCLE OF LEADERSHIP VALOR

The Cycle of Leadership Valor includes four concrete steps that spell out a continual, self-reinforcing process that you can invoke, in whole or in part, over and over again in any situation that calls for you to lead valiantly. These 4 steps are:

Step 1: *Initiate*—Choosing self-awareness.

Step 2: *Illuminate*—Revealing your Three Levels of Reality rather than just what appears to be happening in the moment and recognizing that "Seductions" may be at play.

Step 3: *Curate*—Creating your plan of action and then calibrating your approach as needed.

Step 4: *Integrate*—Reflecting on and incorporating the lessons and wisdom of your experience.

THE THREE LEVELS OF REALITY

As noted in the second step, *Illuminate,* the Leadership Valor approach brings forth "Three Levels of Reality," which you can think of as "worlds" or perspectives:

❖ **Consensus,** or the world of your everyday life. This is what some call the tangible world of the here and now.

❖ **Essence,** or the world that best describes you at your core. This is who you are at your most fundamental level.

❖ **Dreaming,** or the world of aspirations. Whichever term you prefer, this is the part of you that holds what you most want to do and achieve in your work and in your life.

My contention is that as a leader, you are most effective when you are able to access and be present with all of these levels in yourself, rather than just the compelling world of events, problems, and data.

SEDUCTIONS

The second step, *Illuminate*, also invites you to consider six common leadership pitfalls, which I call "Seductions." These are traps that can tempt all of us who serve as leaders. These Seductions offer short-sighted solutions or one-time payoffs, but Seductions can also sabotage who we truly are and where we most want to go. At their worst, they rob us of effectiveness and collegial respect. The Six Leadership Seductions I see most often are:

1. *I Am Right* (Being stuck in your own perspective)

2. *Storytelling* (Creating a distorted reality)

3. *Checking Out* (Choosing to disengage)

4. *Being Distracted* (Paying too much attention to the unimportant)

5. *No!* (Having one answer: No)

6. *It's All About You* (Focusing on everybody else)

USING THIS BOOK AS YOUR GUIDE

 Throughout *Leading Valiantly in Healthcare*, you will find numerous "Guideposts" that offer you specific ways to reflect and practice. Marked with the icon shown here, these sections will help you find and progress on your own path.

Chapters 1-5 conclude with Key Take-Aways, succinct reminders that will help you continue to unlock the valiant leader in you.

You will also read about leaders whose challenges and opportunities are similar to your own. These fictional tales were inspired by the courageous journeys of the many healthcare and nurse leaders I have met over my several decades of leadership development work. To preserve the anonymity of these valiant professionals, the stories here are general representations rather than depictions of actual accounts.

Part I, "Understanding and Claiming Leadership Valor," gives you the background you need to understand and practice leading in this bold, effective way. In Chapter 1, we explore what Leadership Valor is and how it can enhance your leadership. In Chapter 2, we learn what can get in the way of leading valiantly: the Six Leadership Seductions. Chapter 3 covers the Four Steps of Leadership Valor in detail. Part I finishes with Chapter 4, which focuses on preparation: what it takes to follow this path and what you experience when you do.

Part II, "Leading Valiantly in Real Life," gives you an appreciation of leading valiantly by seeing what it looks like "on the ground." This part consists of a series of "Vignettes" and "Perspectives and Tips." These are short pieces that you can read in whatever order you like, depending on your area of interest and the kind of information you are seeking. The "Vignettes" capture real-life situations, invite you to learn from other leaders' stories, and provide exercises and guidelines to help you personalize what you are reading. The

"Perspectives and Tips" offer additional strategies and reflections on the Seductions, the steps, and how to recognize valiant leadership in yourself and others.

Building on the knowledge you have gained in Parts I and II, Part III, "Sustaining Success as a Valiant Leader," begins with Chapter 5 and an in-depth look at how you can customize the cycle and the steps to suit your individual style and needs. Chapter 6 puts it all together. You will step away from the specifics to see what true mastery looks like when you choose to lead with valor, day by day. The book closes with a discussion of the impact you can have on others and the ways you can support your own growth and nurture their development as well.

Leading Valiantly in Healthcare offers you an invitation to see yourself in its stories and its reflections. It describes and calls forth what is brave and valiant in you already. It offers you ways to become more skilled, more grounded, more aware, and more fully connected with yourself. It gives you an approach to become more conscious of, and more satisfied with, your leadership choices. It presents a strategy that you can modify, make your own, and sustain so you can become a master of Leadership Valor.

"Leading Valiantly in Healthcare describes and calls forth what is brave and valiant in you already."

PART I

UNDERSTANDING AND CLAIMING LEADERSHIP VALOR

Our journey of leading valiantly starts with stories, commentary, and reflections that will familiarize you with what valiant leadership is, how it can be derailed, and how it can be claimed, deepened and reclaimed. Chapter 1 defines Leadership Valor, explains the benefits and insights available to you when you choose this path, and offers you perspectives on the valor you already possess. In this chapter, you will also have the opportunity to create a vision of yourself as a fully valiant leader.

Chapter 2 focuses on the Seductions that get in the way of courageous, full-bodied leadership. It describes these unproductive leadership "traps" that start out as natural tendencies but, left unchecked, grow into gripping, robust beliefs and behaviors that undermine and prevent effective leadership. You will learn how these Seductions manifest, and you will consider their costs.

Chapter 3 describes the steps you can take to support yourself as a valiant leader, whether the Seductions are present or not. It discusses each step in the Cycle of Leadership Valor along with the "mini-loop of expediency." Part I concludes with Chapter 4 and a review of what is required to lead valiantly beyond the steps. We will cover readiness, willingness, resistance, practice, and even occasional "failures."

Every chapter includes invitations for you to consider how its stories and observations relate to you. These "Guideposts" are marked "You, Leading Valiantly," and they are designed to offer you opportunities to pause, consider, and apply what you are reading to your own circumstances and challenges.

Let's begin.

1

LEADERSHIP VALOR IN ACTION

I arrived at the executive floor of a large health system and was cordially welcomed by Caroline,* the senior nurse leader who had invited me. I was immediately struck with the strength of Caroline's presence and her genuine warmth. As we walked toward her office, people greeted her with palpable respect. Within those first few minutes, I learned that I was in the company of a solid, focused, and engaging leader. I was beginning to see that Caroline was not only a leader, she was a force.

Her first words anchored her work and her growth in the ensuing months: "Cathy, I want my work to make a difference in the world of healthcare. I feel frustrated in my job; I have reached a plateau in my career, and my boss is fantastic but dependent on my service

---

*As was explained in the introduction, Caroline, like all of the leaders named in this book, is a fictional character inspired by the leaders with whom I have worked and the experiences they have had.

as his right-hand 'man.' I hate to disappoint him, but I am not going to change healthcare if I stay in this job."

As we continued to talk, she shared some of her professional successes in this and previous roles. Her accomplishments were legion, particularly in the areas of improving clinical outcomes and patient care experiences. The metrics attesting to these achievements were truly impressive.

Caroline also talked about her frustrations. Significantly, however, she did not talk about what was not working in her work environment. Instead, she told me about the shortcomings she saw in herself. She felt she was not as successful as she needed to be when faced with too many conflicting priorities. She was not sure she had the proper educational preparation to be credible enough for advancement. She worried that she was overly demanding and sometimes insensitive to others. She also knew she could be swayed by the opinion of others, particularly those she saw as powerful and influential in determining her career progression within the organization.

Caroline invited me to talk confidentially with her co-workers and direct reports. To a person, they offered exemplary and supportive comments about her. To a person, they saw Caroline as a strong, clear, and highly influential leader. To a person, they respected her unwavering focus, her dedication, and her ability to obtain results. Those who reported to her acknowledged that they had to work hard to reach their goals. Yet they did not fault her for adhering to high standards. In fact, they admired her for establishing ambitious but achievable goals.

I compiled these comments without attribution to protect the identity of those who offered them. When Caroline and I reviewed them, she readily acknowledged the disconnect between what people said about her and how she saw herself. Although she took in their opinions with grace, she was still intent on shifting her behavior and her beliefs as needed so she could "make a difference in healthcare."

Over the next few months, she reflected and carefully charted a new future for herself. As she did, she grew even clearer about what was important for her at this stage of her life. She re-evaluated the significance of her long-held pledges to her community, family, religion, and patients. She refreshed her perspective on the essential nature of who she was and what was important in her career. She also became more specific about her vision for changing the world of healthcare.

Caroline gained awareness by thinking differently and by asking herself challenging questions about what was troubling her about this job. She was willing to consider her own role in the problems she was experiencing. In the process, she uncovered flaws in the stories she was telling herself about her level of preparation and how her schooling compared with that of others around her. She was also willing to go a bit deeper and look at the consequences of these stories, including overworking, overperforming, and over-stressing. She knew something had to change.

Soon, Caroline started trying out new practices to shift her focus away from her shortcomings, her boss, and others' viewpoints. While these changes were initially slow to take hold, Caroline eventually made greater and faster strides. Simultaneously, she prepared to speak with her boss about her commitment to serve patients in new ways. As she readied for this conversation, she anchored herself in her own beliefs, values, and aspirations while continuing to be respectful of her boss and his position.

That conversation was successful, despite the difficulty she anticipated. While her boss was upset with the eventuality of her departure, he understood and ultimately supported her ambitions.

When I last saw Caroline, she was settling into a new position. Significantly, she had taken a job that others considered a step down. Caroline, however, saw her new job as just the opportunity she wanted: This was her chance to make a difference in the world of healthcare. As I left her, it was clear to me that Caroline was already establishing herself as a force in her new role. She was well on her way to making her dream a reality.

As you step back from Caroline's story, consider whether there are aspects of her journey that are similar to your own. Are there parts of her story that inspire you? If so, which ones? Consider whether you, too, have barriers that hinder you at times. Think about whether you, too, have a leadership goal that is deeply important to you. It does not have to be epic in scope like Caroline's; it can be as simple as achieving smoother working relationships or reducing costs on the unit. In fact, your goal might change from day to day. Or, perhaps it is obscured by your many responsibilities and the rigors of your daily life.

If you relate to any part of Caroline's story, know that you are not alone. It is not uncommon for healthcare stewards at all levels to have difficulty realizing their true aspirations amid the many demands of their professional lives. Yet leaders like Caroline and leaders like you can and do find satisfying ways to surmount barriers and integrate into their working lives who they truly are and what they most want to achieve.

> ### BEING VALIANT
>
> "Your leadership goal does not have to be epic in scope like Caroline's; it can be as simple as achieving smoother working relationships or reducing costs."

I see this way of leading as courageous and "valiant." In this chapter, you will learn what valiant leadership is and how to access and tailor it so you can lead in ways that are more satisfying, less stressful, and more sustainable.

WHAT IS LEADERSHIP VALOR?

You can begin to understand Leadership Valor by noticing the actions and qualities that helped Caroline achieve her goal despite the obstacles she experienced:

❖ She drew on a state of being that was already within her. She was willing to dream and aspire; she was very clear from day one that she wanted "to make a difference in the world of healthcare."

❖ She knew something was off, and she wanted to think differently about what was happening.

❖ She was ready to let in new information so she could learn, and she was willing let go of old habits and beliefs that were in the way.

❖ She asked herself hard questions, and she reflected on her answers, even when they were uncomfortable.

❖ She updated her view of herself by considering whether what had been important in the past was still important in the present.

❖ Although she was not happy with the imperfections she saw in herself, she was willing to address or accept them.

❖ She was aware of her heart as well as her mind. She was guided by staying true to herself and her ambitions, even when others did not agree with her choices.

As you review the specific behaviors and qualities that Caroline demonstrates, you can see that she was keenly aware of and motivated by an unwavering internal sense of who she was, what she wanted, and what she could do to achieve her deeply held goals. She was willing to explore places in herself that needed to be updated and refreshed. She was also willing to behave differently and adjust her attitudes when they were unproductive. In other words, she was willing to practice new behaviors and let go of beliefs, stories, and attitudes that were not serving her. All of these are examples of leading valiantly.

LEADERSHIP VALOR IS...

Leadership Valor is a state of being and doing in which a leader:

- ❖ Exhibits bravery
- ❖ Acts with integrity
- ❖ Stays clear and focused
- ❖ Is committed to increasing self-awareness
- ❖ Is able to learn, grow, and change
- ❖ Is willing to practice new behaviors
- ❖ Can release attitudes and "stories" that no longer serve

WHY CALL IT LEADERSHIP "VALOR"?

The word "valor" may surprise you. Why would I use a word that is so often associated with heroism in both men and women? The reason: I regularly witness healthcare leaders who exemplify the traits commonly associated with bravery:

- ❖ Character
- ❖ Honesty
- ❖ Fortitude
- ❖ Grace

- ❖ Principled
- ❖ Purposeful
- ❖ Confident
- ❖ Inspired

Yet as accurate and appropriate as these words are, they do not define the whole of Leadership Valor. Valiant leaders are also:

- ❖ Grounded, clear, and centered

- ❖ Self-aware

- ❖ Willing to reflect and to learn

- ❖ Able to contemplate the part they play in their problems and challenges

- ❖ Able to recover from errors in judgment and mistakes

- ❖ Vulnerable on occasion

- ❖ Flexible and open to new information

- ❖ Willing to change course when advisable

WHAT ABOUT YOU?

How does this leadership stance resonate for you? When you read the preceding lists and reflect on the questions in the Guidepost that follows, how do you see yourself? Imagine that you have a challenge or opportunity that requires your best. Consider the earlier short-hand descriptions of Leadership Valor and think about whether these characteristics apply to you.

Note that Leadership Valor is not about leading in this way 100% of the time. Admirable as that would be, it is a largely unattainable state. Instead, mastering Leadership Valor is about leading this way more frequently. The question is, how can you define, embrace, and integrate these qualities so they work for you on a sustainable basis?

How can your unique version of Leadership Valor bolster you to move ahead with greater clarity, satisfaction, and resolve?

YOU, LEADING VALIANTLY

1. Think about an opportunity or challenge that you have right now.

2. Consider how the characteristics of Leadership Valor can assist you in dealing successfully with the opportunity or challenge you have identified.

INTEGRITY AND LEADERSHIP VALOR

When you reflect on the characteristics associated with Leadership Valor, note that many are rooted in your personal well-being and your integrity. Integrity is indeed central to this form of leadership. It is also foundational to how people view effectiveness in the healthcare stewards around them. This was a key conclusion in my gender-focused research study and subsequent book titled *Women and Leadership in Health Care: The Journey to Authenticity and Power* (Robinson-Walker, 1999). That book contained a significant finding: Regardless of the gender of the leader, integrity is the single most important factor in perceived leadership effectiveness by both women and men in healthcare.

> *"Integrity is the single most important factor in perceived leadership effectiveness by both women and men in healthcare."*

But what does integrity really look like today in the fast-paced, über-complex world of healthcare? We see in Caroline an example not only of Leadership Valor, but also, and not coincidentally, a leader who demonstrates full-bodied integrity. She exhibits a kind of personal wholeness and professional congruence that any leader—including you—can summon to serve as the foundation for your own leadership journey.

This is a kind of integrity that builds on abiding principles, beliefs, and commitments while also acknowledging that there are occasions that require shifts in perception, focus, and direction. These changes may be substantial or modest, or anything in between.

Caroline's story opens this chapter because in it she displays a rich, multidimensional version of who she was. She was clear about what she wanted, yet she was also fully attuned to what was in the way. She was willing to pursue deeper self-understanding and a different future, even as her colleagues sang her praises and held a vision of a better path to advancement than she herself sought.

Caroline's actions tell us that she knows she must serve as the conscious steward of herself and her own leadership growth. Like many good leaders, Caroline knows she must remain skilled in the technical aspects of her craft and enhance her leadership knowledge on a regular basis. But Caroline sees her responsibility to grow as more than acquiring additional knowledge and skill. Significantly, she believes it is her job to remain awake and present not only to her competence, but also to the external events that are influencing her and to what is happening inside her mind, heart, and even her dreams for achievement.

Those around Caroline said she was an engaging, highly influential, and inspiring leader with a natural and seemingly effortless presence. Uniformly, her co-workers commented on their ability to trust in her word, her judgment, and her vision. Caroline's colleagues were expressing their experience of her integrity and her valiant leadership.

Notice the difference between what Caroline's colleagues saw in her and what she saw in herself. Even after learning about their enduring respect for her as a leader, she was not content to set aside her concerns. As happy as she was about their feedback, it did not dissuade her from the important work of sorting out how to achieve her dream. In short, Caroline was committing to leading with valor, as described in Table 1.1.

TABLE 1.1 WITHOUT VALOR, WITH VALOR: COMPARING LEADERSHIP APPROACHES

Leading Without Valor	Leading With Valor
We see leadership as a static process that is: ❖ Usually the same ❖ Not wholly or consciously connected with who we are, who we want to be, and what we most want to achieve	We see leadership as a dynamic process that expresses in the right measure our skill, our aspirations, and our essence as a human being. As such our leadership: ❖ Evolves ❖ Is responsive to who we are, where we are, and what's going on around us ❖ Acknowledges and manages the dual requirements of leadership consistency and leadership flexibility
We strive for perfection and are deeply disappointed when we do not achieve it.	We lead with a redefined notion of excellence as "better and better."
We react to most situations in similar ways.	We respond thoughtfully, fully, and individually to situations when they are unusual and/or particularly important.

Leading Without Valor	Leading With Valor
We operate on the principle that if we work harder, we'll succeed, and people will probably acknowledge and thank us.	We work in a way that honors who we are and who we want to be, so that our work: ❖ Allows us to shine more often ❖ Supports rather than drains us ❖ Allows us to be genuinely inspired and motivated rather than looking to others to build us up
We work to live up to other people's definitions of leadership success.	We define and focus on achieving success on our own terms while honoring the importance of our professional and organizational standards for success.
We make a decision and stick with it, regardless of how circumstances evolve and what new information we glean.	We adjust our leadership strategies based on new circumstances, additional information, and new learning. We practice and try new approaches when we think they are best, even if they are new to us or difficult to implement.
We quickly move on when our work is "done" and situations are resolved.	We are committed to learning from our experiences through conscious reflection and integration (whether that reflection is for a short moment or a long time).

continues

TABLE 1.1   WITHOUT VALOR, WITH VALOR:
COMPARING LEADERSHIP APPROACHES   *(CONTINUED)*

Leading Without Valor	Leading With Valor
We see ourselves as possessing a fixed set of leadership "assets," including competencies, skills, and abilities. We see ourselves as novices, advanced beginners, competent, proficient, or experts in most or all tasks.	We believe that our leadership "assets" grow and evolve. As we learn, practice, and develop our way of leading, we add to, nourish, and change some of these assets. We let others fall away when they no longer serve us and/or others. We acknowledge that while we may be experts in some aspects of leadership, we may be novices in others.

LEADERSHIP VALOR AND YOU

Exemplary as Caroline's journey is, this book is not about Caroline. It is about you. It is about offering you examples, stories, practices, exercises, and reflective questions that will assist you as you make Leadership Valor your own. It is about making your day-to-day life as a leader more successful, more satisfying, and more sustainable. It is about honoring the part of you that legendary dancer and choreographer Martha Graham described to Agnes de Mille:

> There is a vitality, a life force, a quickening that is translated through you into action, and because there is only one of you in all time, this expression is unique. And if you block it, it will never exist through any other medium and it will be lost. (de Mille, 1991, p. 264)

If you allow this part of yourself, your life force, to remain hidden or unexpressed, you won't live into the fullest expression of who you can be. And without you and the fulfillment you can achieve, healthcare cannot evolve. The system cannot afford to lose you and the best you can offer. In fact, it can survive and thrive only if you survive and thrive, too.

"The system cannot afford to lose you and the best you can offer. In fact, it can survive and thrive only if you survive and thrive, too."

Compelling as that single fact is, there are still more reasons to go on the Leadership Valor journey. The following sections describe those that are most important.

YOU, AS LEADER, MANAGER, OR PROVIDER

As a leader, manager, clinician, worker, or aspiring student, you are joining with others to do nothing short of transforming the health-care system. Directly or indirectly, your work is to serve patients and communities. This calling has always demanded your best, and now is no exception. Leadership Valor offers an attainable, memorable process along with a series of steps that can provide you with greater access to your own wisdom, skill, and motivation so you can do the work demanded of you every day.

You, Continuing to Learn

Many leaders want to stay current in their fields, act on positive personal goals, and simply take care of themselves. Yet these same leaders often find it difficult to accomplish these things and build habits that support their own leadership excellence and good health. They just don't have the time to do what it takes to care for themselves and also learn as they should.

Unfortunately, the consequences of not tending to professional and personal well-being are serious. Depleted leaders may hold onto old leadership positions and philosophies too tightly and too long, whether that's for a few hours or a few years or more. This way of leading promotes inertia, decay, and ignorance not only in them but also in those around them. When leaders demonstrate this kind of stagnation, however unwittingly, these same unhealthy qualities can also characterize their teams and possibly even their organizations.

The reality is that poorly managed leaders' lives can become significant barriers that keep other leaders and managers from being their most effective, too. When on the job, overworked or overwhelmed leaders may be unable and unwilling to take in new information, reflect on it, evaluate it, and appropriately adjust their statements and behaviors. These inadvertent but potent ways of showing up at work can shut down innovation, communication, and progress at all levels of the system.

Poet and speaker David Whyte (2002) says that as we go on in life, we find the larger sense of ourselves. Leadership Valor posits that you and I will evolve into greater and greater versions of ourselves *if we attend to our own growth*. We will evolve into this state if we allow ourselves to consciously change, and if we permit ourselves to take in the new and release that which no longer serves us or others. Leadership Valor offers a way to practice taking in and releasing so that we can grow into that "larger sense of ourselves" as leaders and as human beings.

YOU, DEDICATED TO WHAT MATTERS MOST

Leadership Valor is not about someone else's idea of what you should be focused on and dedicated to at your place of work. Instead, it offers a way for you to remember or identify anew who you are today, what you most want to achieve in your work and, if you like, in your life. From the Leadership Valor vantage point, what matters is that the foundation of your leadership is robust, self-defined, and focused on your authentic immediate, long-term, and heartfelt goals.

YOU, MAXIMIZING YOUR IMPACT AND EFFECTIVENESS

Leadership Valor is as much about looking at yourself as it is about being keenly aware of—and able to relate effectively to—what is going on around you. Caroline's colleagues described what it is like for a leader to have a deep and abiding impact on others when that leader is viewed as immanently trustworthy. They spoke about her ways of inspiring and motivating them with unflinching respect.

While we know that Caroline was deeply concerned about her own imperfections, she managed these perceived insufficiencies so they did not detract from her ability to be fully present with her co-workers. Practicing Leadership Valor allows you to attend to what must be addressed within yourself while also being able to shift your focus to others when needed.

Leadership Valor prepares you to become a better teacher and mentor, whether or not you formally hold those roles. The need for skilled guides has never been greater. Many new and inexperienced healthcare workers will enter the field to meet healthcare demands that will explode as baby boomers age and require increasing amounts of care.

You, Inspired

Leaders soar when they are operating from their own brand of Leadership Valor. Caroline is one example; Jesse is another:

> *Jesse was invited to give "the speech of her life" as the new CEO of a national organization. As she tells it, she prepared well and knew her "stuff" cold; she was very excited and very committed. She was connected with and believed in herself, her message, and her audience. Her success with the speech turned out to be a high point for Jesse for at least the next year and perhaps longer. It also gave her a fully alive memory of how she could be as a leader. Getting to that effortless level of delivery required hard work, but the benefit was enormous and long lasting.*

As you have seen, the practice of Leadership Valor promotes greater congruence between who you truly are as a leader and human being and what you are working toward every day. It is first and foremost a way of experiencing yourself: of being brave enough to show up amid uncertainty; aware enough to make conscious, often difficult choices; and deliberate enough to face what is not working and address it so you can be more effective.

> ### BEING VALIANT
>
> "Leadership Valor is first and foremost a way of experiencing yourself: of being brave enough to show up amid uncertainty; aware enough to make conscious, often difficult choices; and deliberate enough to face what is not working and address it so you can be more effective."

YOU, NOURISHED

Incorporating these practices into your life and work will allow you to experience more peace and resilience along with less stress and frustration. When your beliefs, statements, strategies, and actions are rooted not only in skillful leadership practices, but also in who you are and what you most want to accomplish, you will be more congruent with the whole of who you are when you are on the job. This alignment creates a state of fulfillment that is simply not present when you are buffeted about by circumstances; other people's attitudes, opinions, and agendas; and even your own lack of self-care.

When you are nourished, you can be deeply connected with your personal and professional power. Nurtured and grounded leaders who are firmly rooted in their own sensibilities are able to be present for others, operate with more fortitude, and influence with the full impact of their vision and strength.

Leadership Valor can, quite simply, help you reconnect with your humanity. In the rush for success and professional survival, all of us can disconnect from that which makes us most vital. Leadership Valor provides a process for personal and professional reconnection with who you are and who you want to be at your professional best.

YOU, IN ACTION

All leaders are challenged, and at times, all leaders find themselves in patches of emotional discomfort when something just doesn't feel right. If this happens to you, you may blame others, a bad situation, or yourself. And, at times, you may not really know what is causing the angst.

The practice of leading valiantly allows you to find your way back. It offers a path to self-awareness that is rooted in what is true and real for you. While taking the journey to self-knowledge can be arduous, it doesn't have to be. You can make this approach as easy or challenging as you wish.

A clear vision of the leader you most want to be will serve as a powerful touchstone for you in any situation. The next Guidepost walks you through a process of creating your vision. Over the course of the book, you will be invited to recall and refine it so that it precisely fits you and your unique opportunities and challenges.

YOU, LEADING VALIANTLY

1. Imagine yourself as the valiant leader you are capable of being.

2. Next, capture what you see and create your vision of yourself.
    Fill in as much detail as you can, considering the following
    questions. (Use a journal to write your answers if you like.)
    Take the time you need to think about your answers. If you are
    moved to share them with others, do so.

    ❖ What outcomes will you be able to achieve when you lead
       more valiantly, more often?

    ❖ What qualities will be the same, and what will be different
       about you when you lead this way?

    ❖ What behaviors will you engage in more frequently than
       you do now? What behaviors will you engage in less often?

    ❖ What adjectives describe how you will handle the everyday
       opportunities and challenges of your job? Some possibilities
       are: creative, bold, courageous, risk-taking, etc.

    ❖ How do you feel about yourself when you envision yourself
       leading in this way on a more consistent basis?

3. Select or create an object to serve as a symbol of your vision of
    yourself as a valiant leader. It can be a photograph or piece of
    art, a poem or book, a memento from a success or special time
    in your life, a piece of jewelry, a note from someone who appre-
    ciated your efforts, a personal item—anything. It can even be a
    word or saying. Keep it where you can see it often as a reminder
    of your vision.

Closing Thoughts

As you become familiar with, practice, and adapt Leadership Valor so that it suits you and your unique circumstances, you will begin to experience its many benefits. Still, simple and attainable as valiant leadership is, there are some barriers or "derailers" that can get in the way. These are our natural tendencies to become too attached to attitudes and strategies that just don't work. Most of these tendencies start out being normal and natural, but at some point, they turn into major obstructions because they become overblown. I call these roadblocks "Leadership Seductions." They're just ahead in Chapter 2.

KEY TAKE-AWAYS

❖ Leadership Valor is a state of being and doing. When leading valiantly, a leader exemplifies bravery, clarity, focus, openness, self-awareness, flexibility, and the willingness to learn, grow, change, and practice.

❖ Leadership Valor is rooted in integrity. It builds on abiding principles, beliefs, and aspirations while also acknowledging that there are occasions that require shifts in perception, focus, and direction.

❖ When you lead with valor in a way that uniquely suits you, you make your day-to-day life as a leader more satisfying, less stressful, and more sustainable.

❖ Valiant leaders continue to learn, grow, and maximize their impact and effectiveness. They are clear about and dedicated to what matters most.

❖ Your vision of the leader you most want to be will serve as a powerful touchstone for you in any situation.

2

VALOR INTERRUPTED: LEADERSHIP SEDUCTIONS AND THEIR IMPACT

As you read these brief stories about your fellow healthcare leaders, do any of them resonate with you?

❖ *Rose is locked in a disagreement with her peers about ways to bring their team together, and she is certain her approach is best. They have been at odds for several weeks, and she will not entertain the options others are offering. As the conflict continues, their previously strong working relationships are fraying.*

❖ *George received a lot of positive feedback in his written and oral performance reviews. Yet he is focused on a few small suggestions for improvement, and he feels terrible about his failings.*

❖ *For years, Jordan wanted to go back to school for a doctoral degree, but her husband and some of her co-workers discouraged her. Her organization recently implemented a new policy that would help her with the tuition, but she declined to apply for the next session of school.*

❖ *Ginny is a senior leader, and her colleagues and direct reports rely on her clarity and guidance. However, Ginny is not keeping up. She spends hours and hours on email, and she finds it increasingly difficult to stay on top of the many meetings and other demands that are placed upon her.*

❖ *Monique appears to be in a perpetually negative frame of mind. She is a manager on a complex unit with three other managers, and whenever they brainstorm ways to improve their services and address their area's deficiencies, she shoots down every idea.*

❖ *Louise is very annoyed with her boss and his explanations about why he cannot give her the additional resources she needs. In passing, she has requested more staff support several times. She can't stop thinking about how ill-prepared he is for his position, and she fantasizes about telling his boss about his failings.*

Do you see any parallels between these leaders' challenges and your own? If so, welcome to the world of Leadership Seductions. These are the all-too-easy traps that you and I and every other healthcare leader can fall into on occasion. These are just a few examples of the behaviors and beliefs that give us solace when things are not going our way. These are the perspectives that might make us feel better in the short run because we can say, "It's her fault," or even, "He doesn't know what he's doing."

While these ordinary, everyday coping strategies might comfort you and me in the moment, we know they are not long-lasting solutions to the serious requirements of leadership now. Yet, in my experience of working with healthcare and nurse leaders, I find that many of us engage in at least mild versions of one or more of these patterns that I call "Seductions." Being taken by a Seduction or two from time to time is not bad; it is entirely human. The problem, however, is that by their nature, Seductions are "side trips" that don't take us where we want to go.

Leading with valor does not mean you are Seduction-free. Knowing about and understanding the power of Leadership Seductions will not give you immunity to them. However, the knowledge you will gain in this chapter will equip you so you will recognize them when they occur. You will know what the Seductions can do, not only to you but also to those around you. The purpose of this exploration is to introduce you to these Seductions and reveal how they manifest for leaders like you. As tempting as it is to offer quick-fix solutions to the Seductions at this point, this chapter instead grounds you by providing discussion, examples, and reflections for you to consider. You will find workable approaches, perspectives, and tips for addressing and managing the Seductions in subsequent parts of this book, including Chapters 3 and 5, and in the first half of Part II.

"Being taken by a Seduction or two from time to time is entirely human."

WHAT EXACTLY IS A LEADERSHIP SEDUCTION?

Seduction is a provocative word that is not usually used in a professional context. Yet it is a fitting description for a potent enticement. A Leadership Seduction is a powerful "hook," usually an unconscious temptation, habit, or operating strategy that is not helpful in the current situation. A Seduction can kick in all too quickly when we as leaders are not at our best, and when we are confronted with difficulties we can't or don't want to face. The scenarios at the beginning of this chapter are all examples of the Seductions discussed in this book; the capital "S" differentiates these from traditional seductions that have a different and broader connotation.

"A Leadership Seduction is a powerful 'hook,' usually an unconscious temptation, habit, or operating strategy that is not helpful in the current situation."

YOU, LEADING VALIANTLY

HOW DO YOU KNOW IF YOU ARE EXPERIENCING A LEADERSHIP SEDUCTION?

You can suspect you are experiencing a Leadership Seduction when you have an encounter and you have some or all of the following reactions:

- ❖ Your reaction feels "triggered."

- ❖ Your response is strong and immediate.

- ❖ You find it difficult to stop thinking about the situation— you might even say you are fixated on it.

- ❖ Your internal or external reaction lets you escape from an unpleasant perspective, at least for a while.

- ❖ Your response gives you a small (or large) moment of emotional relief, satisfaction, or even a "payoff."

- ❖ Your comfort does not last and there is a price. Perhaps you don't have a needed conversation with a co-worker, you don't go back to school, or you don't rectify the stories you are telling yourself that are undermining your relationship with your boss.

- ❖ You notice that you respond similarly to a variety of situations.

- ❖ You (perhaps secretly) like to enroll other people in this probably negative point of view.

We might say that Leadership Seductions are behaviors or attitudes in which we become "stuck." In other words, we become attached to these ill-serving coping strategies. Seductions really are "sticky" because they can be quite difficult to shake off. In fact, we may not *want* to shake them off. Even when we become conscious of our Seductions, we may still indulge in them because they are guilty pleasures that we just don't want to give up.

It is important to note that not every example of a behavior or attitude that is related to the six Seductions is a full-fledged Seduction. Fleeting behaviors, attitudes, feelings, and even "bad moods" do not qualify as Seductions. However, they can become Seductions when we experience them frequently and with a level of intensity that is distinctly different from using these coping strategies once in a while, for a brief period, and in a much diluted form. For example, think about times when you have caught yourself blaming someone else, but then quickly self-corrected after you realized there was more to consider. Pointing the finger at someone else once in a while is human and does not qualify as a Seduction. It is merely an example of a momentary indulgence. In other words, the behavior is not a long-term habit, out of proportion, or particularly intense. It's just a thought that comes, goes, and does not interfere with leading valiantly. Keep this concept of intensity in mind as you read the following descriptions and consider if Seductions are operating for you.

This exploration of Seductions is not intended to be an indictment or a deep psychological analysis. Here, we are not interested in all of the historical, psycho-social reasons that could explain these temptations. Instead, we are interested in the Seductions because they serve as significant barriers to leading with valor. What we want to focus on is that we *are* tempted, that we *do* succumb, and that often, there are negative consequences if we don't relinquish these Seductions.

WHO IS SUSCEPTIBLE TO SEDUCTIONS?

Nearly all leaders are susceptible to Seductions. Why? Because nearly all of us have a lot to attend to, move fast, and operate as street-savvy human beings who do not have time to carefully consider every important circumstance that requires a response. Nearly all of us need more down time than we get, more reflection opportunity than we have, and more self-care than we allow. This state of affairs is not "bad"; it just *is*.

"Nearly all of us need more down time than we get, more reflection opportunity than we have, and more self-care than we allow. This state of affairs is not 'bad'; it just is."

Although Seductions are universal, we are not powerless in facing them. We have a choice to learn about, understand, and consider whether one or more of the Leadership Seductions is influencing us. And if one is, we can decide what to do about it. The point of this exploration is not to suggest that we are wrong when we succumb. The point is to shed light on these temptations and to understand their costs so we can choose to yield or not.

How Do Leaders Experience These Seductions?

Unfortunately, Seductions rarely show up in an isolated form. In fact, they usually occur in groups, or "clusters," as some of the Vignettes in Part II, "Leading Valiantly in Real Life," show. When they do, there is usually one primary Seduction that drives the others. In the descriptions of Seductions that follow, however, they are defined separately so you can explore them one by one. As you begin to consider whether Seductions influence you, you will notice that the discrete lines that divide them here are far more blurred in real life.

When you read these descriptions, remember that we each understand Leadership Seductions from our own unique perspective. You may see a Seduction from one standpoint, and I might see it from another. There is no one right way; however you describe a Seduction is what is true for you. Whether we like it or not, when we are stuck in these traps, each of us creates and embodies our own unique version of the Leadership Seductions.

YOU, LEADING VALIANTLY

1. Take your time as you read the descriptions of Seductions in the remainder of this chapter:

   ❖ Consider whether any of these Seductions occasionally operate for you. If they do, ask yourself when they do and what happens when they do?

   ❖ Ask yourself whether they are momentary or more permanent detours that take you away from you at your best.

2. What are the consequences of being "stuck" in one or more Seductions?

3. Consider the costs to you and to those around you.

THE SIX LEADERSHIP SEDUCTIONS

Figure 2.1 displays the Leadership Seductions that occur over and over again. While they do not encompass the entire universe of possible Seductions, these six Seductions are the patterns that get in the way most often when leaders—and perhaps you—would like to lead valiantly but can't quite make it happen.

FIGURE 2.1   SIX LEADERSHIP SEDUCTIONS

SEDUCTION 1   *I Am Right*

The long version of *I Am Right* is, "I am utterly and completely attached to my idea, my point of view, and/or my emotional reaction. It is true and 'right,' and I will not change it, no matter what." Notice the strident quality of this statement. Note, too, that the long version is not something we actually say in so many words. We may not even be aware of our over-the-top attachment to our point of view. However, our responses still convey this message.

In its righteousness, this Seduction communicates its wholly unchanging nature, *even when there might be an internal stirring or external evidence that another perspective is equally valid or better.* This

Seduction is about being stuck in one perspective. It is about inflexibility and unwillingness to let emotions pass, to let new information in, and/or to consider different points of view. At its most extreme, according to Marshall Goldsmith (2007), leaders can be so taken with their stories, beliefs, emotions, values, etc., that they actually *are* those things.

To resist this Seduction does not mean that we give up our identity, our feelings, or our measured positions on a whim. It does mean, however, that we are open to a different point of view. Leadership Valor is, in part, about being present to what's new and what may require flexibility. It's difficult to lead valiantly when we are stuck in a version of *I Am Right*.

"Leadership Valor is, in part, about being present to what's new and what may require flexibility. It's difficult to lead valiantly when we are stuck in a version of I Am Right."

An example of this Seduction started this chapter:

> *Rose is locked in a disagreement with her peers about ways to bring their team together, and she is certain her approach is best. They have been at odds for several weeks, and she will not entertain the options others are offering. As the conflict continues, their previously strong working relationships are fraying.*

There are many other versions of this Seduction. Just a few are:

❖ "I am an expert, and I wear my expert hat in every situation, *even if it doesn't apply, is overblown, or otherwise inappropriate in those situations.* I will not or do not see indications that my expertise may not be relevant or wanted. I am not able to dial it back when my knowledge and experience do not add value."

❖ "I often say to myself or out loud, *'That's just the way I am,'* even in the face of a compelling need to alter or at least temporarily adjust my stance."

❖ "If people don't agree with me, it is so difficult for me to take in their perspectives that I can't listen. As a result, I am caught off guard at times: I don't see the trouble that is brewing. When that happens, my co-workers are not as surprised as I am; they say I could have seen it coming."

The Cost of I Am Right

One consequence of this Seduction is that leaders who communicate this world view can send a double message. The first is that they are right and their answer is the best (and only) answer. The second is that a different point of view is wrong. In other words, the underlying message associated with *I Am Right* is "You are wrong." Or, "I am better (than you are)," or, "I am more important (than you are)." Predictably, the receivers of the *I Am Right* message hear that they are wrong, worse, or less important.

Other potential consequences of *I Am Right* are:

❖ This virulent, steadfast point of view may be a leadership blind spot. By definition, that means entrenched leaders can't see it but others can. (They "know" they are experts in scope of practice, for instance, but others know they have not kept up-to-date with the latest dialogue about regulations.)

❖ Leaders who are locked into how they perceive themselves may not see that others are tuning them out. Why do others tune them out? Because the other people already know where these leaders stand. There's no point in listening to them.

❖ Leaders stuck in *I Am Right* are often seen as overly serious, inflexible, and unable to learn. They may also be defensive.

❖ These leaders may have a heavy-handed approach with other people and little to no sense of humor.

SEDUCTION 2 *Storytelling*

Storytelling is easiest to understand by imagining an overly simple view of the world that is divided into two parts: actual events and our interpretation of those events. As human beings we directly experience the world around us and our internal lives, and then we interpret them. Through our interpretations, we make meaning out of our experiences. The meaning we make, and the stories we tell ourselves and others about that meaning, can become a leadership vulnerability or a Seduction.

Storytelling involves a distorted account of an actual external or internal experience. All interpretations are by definition "made up," but the stories that fall within this Seduction's range are *far less* accurate accounts of facts and occurrences; they may be exaggerated, minimized, or wholly different versions of those occurrences. Note that the emphasis here is on "far less." While "far less" is a subjective term, you can make it meaningful by considering whether you are (unwittingly) telling erroneous stories to yourself and/or others.

This Seduction is not the same thing as the constant internal dialogue most of us carry on in our waking moments. This is our "chatter," and it is simply that: We are just talking to ourselves. *Storytelling* kicks in when the chatter amplifies, we build on it, and suddenly, we have created—and are attached to—a new reality that no longer closely approximates the actual experience, the evidence, or the facts.

An example of *Storytelling* comes from the leader who says to herself, "They don't like or support me," when the facts strongly suggest that story is simply not true. Despite receiving a lot of support, this leader may have experienced an insignificant slight or a trivial behavior that was unfriendly and unsupportive. With just that small shred of evidence, the leader ensnares herself in a much bigger story. Because she is stuck in the Seduction (the "big" story she concocted), she is living in, and probably acting on, a perspective that unnecessarily discourages and disempowers her.

A similar example of this Seduction is the story that appeared at the beginning of this chapter:

> *George received a lot of positive feedback in his written and oral performance reviews. Yet he is focused on a few small suggestions for improvement, and he feels terrible about his failings.*

George is fixated on a few opportunities for improvement in an otherwise exemplary performance review. He is calling them "failings" and sending a message to himself and anyone he is talking with that he is unsuccessful. Notice the impact of this Seduction: George is literally making himself feel badly, and it is a direct result of the exaggerated story he is telling himself.

There are many other versions of this Seduction. Just a few are:

- ❖ **The story of one's own importance.** Even as it plays out unconsciously, this story can become a leadership favorite. There are lots of variations on this story. Sometimes leaders simply take too much credit for team or organizational successes. Alternatively, leaders may slide into stories about being the cause of problems that have little or nothing to do with them.

- ❖ **The story of scarcity.** This can take many forms such as "There is not enough," "I am not enough," "You are not enough," "I am not young enough, not old enough, not smart enough," and so on.

- ❖ **The story of egos.** A still different version of *Storytelling* occurs with some leaders who have large egos (and equally big stories) that are spawned by the trappings of their roles, their substantial salaries, their bigger staffs, and all the people who say "yes" to them. In each of these cases, it takes an aware—and valiant—leader to escape this Seduction and stay awake and grounded.

The Cost of Storytelling

There are as many consequences for this Seduction as there are for not telling the truth, whether inadvertently or deliberately. For instance, an internal story of scarcity may invite self-pity and taking the stance of a victim. It may also invite:

❖ Giving personal power away

❖ Exaggerating one's importance

❖ Minimizing one's own efforts

❖ Feeling badly about oneself

❖ Inaction or "checking out" (described in Seduction 3: *Checking Out*)

The most critical consequence for leaders is that they are seriously misrepresenting reality for themselves and for others. Leaders and managers who are taken with *Storytelling* are excessively distorting what they report to those around them: their direct reports, their bosses, and their peers. They may not be consciously changing, minimizing, or exaggerating how bad or good things are, but they are also not working to consciously portray an accurate version of events. Whether their distortions are intentional or not, the consequences of their misrepresentations are just as serious.

It is important to understand these costs in the larger context of Leadership Valor and its foundation of your integrity. One of the most essential aspects of your job as a leader is the thoughtful and accurate retelling of events and "reality" for those around you. The words you use and the way you describe what you see create the working world that your peers, co-workers, direct reports, and others respond to, live in, and experience. In short, you and other leaders do not just *describe* reality, you *create* it, too. This is an enormous responsibility, and it is one that requires the best you can offer.

"You and other leaders do not just describe reality, you create it, too. This is an enormous responsibility, and it is one that requires the best you can offer."

SEDUCTION 3 *Checking Out*

Checking Out is about living, but only halfway. We know that this Seduction has taken hold in its most obvious state when a leader appears to be resigned or disengaged. Such an individual leads by habit, responds the same way in most situations, and shows up at meetings with little or nothing to offer. This leader is often (but not always) negative, too. This leader has lost zest, freshness, passion, and vitality.

This description offers the view of a checked-out leader in a fairly extreme form. But remember that this Seduction, like all of them, can come in less virulent forms, too. A leader who is angry or frustrated may check out, but just for a short time. Valiant leaders won't let being "checked out" for a while become a Seduction. Instead, they will identify the source of their upset and decide what to do about it. They will address it sooner rather than later so they can opt back in to full-bodied, valiant stewardship.

But leaders who are *perpetually* tired, grumpy, apathetic, and/or unwilling to change may be *Checked Out*, and not just for a while. As noted, leaders who started with *Storytelling* can also check out. What puts these leaders squarely in the category of *Checking Out* is that their stories are remarkably similar and long-lasting. These stories often amount to "It won't work," or "I can't." These checked-out leaders can also be described as *tuned-out* leaders. That means their filters are operating full tilt, and if anything is getting through, it is probably a story-laden myth about why "It's not worth it."

An example of a leader who has checked out is Jordan, whose story you read at the beginning of this chapter:

> *For years, Jordan wanted to go back to school for a doctoral degree, but her husband and some of her co-workers discouraged her. Her organization recently implemented a new policy that would help her with the tuition, but she declined to apply for the next session of school.*

Jordan has not only checked out; it appears that she has also given up her dream. This is a significant loss for her, and it is likely to impact her spirit, her motivation, and her success for a long time.

Leaders taken by other variations of *Checking Out* may:

❖ Not live up to their full potential. This could be because they are discouraged, afraid to be successful, afraid of failure, or anything in between.

❖ Feel and act like they are "imposters." They may have all the training they need, they may be recognized for their skills and abilities, or they may even be seen as experts. No matter what the evidence tells them and others about their competence, these leaders don't own it.

❖ Take in stories and information without discernment. They may abdicate their responsibilities to listen for what is important and to act valiantly when something needs to be challenged, distilled, passed on, or implemented.

❖ Sit in the passenger seat when they, their teams, and their organizations would be better served by the stronger input they could contribute.

The Cost of Checking Out

Like all the Seductions, behaviors associated with *Checking Out* are costly to healthcare leaders and their organizations. Some of these costs are:

❖ A great deal of talent and productivity is lost in organizations when leaders disengage.

❖ Younger, less-experienced clinicians, managers, and leaders see how these leaders operate on the job. They are influenced by checked-out behavior and its consequences. They also notice when neither the leader nor the organization does anything about it. Unfortunately, the only question is *how* these younger leaders will be influenced, not *whether* they will be influenced.

❖ Checked-out leaders are usually not motivated to create what is new and needed on the job.

Valiant leadership is about "stepping up." Leaders who are checked out don't usually step up. The organizations suffer, the patients suffer, and countless others do not benefit from the talent and possibility these leaders keep to themselves.

SEDUCTION 4: *Being Distracted*

Being Distracted refers to succumbing too often to the alluring and overwhelming attraction of the unimportant. The operative words here are "too often." As leaders, we can make a good case for doing lighter but necessary management tasks throughout the day. We can actually be refreshed when we take care of routine business, such as spending a few minutes looking through emails and texts, returning phone calls, and reading reports that are important but not urgent.

Distraction that is a healthy change of pace in a busy leader's life is not what this Seduction is about. This Seduction is about spending excessive amounts of time on insignificant pastimes and costly time-wasters.

Like all of the Seductions, *Being Distracted* can take many forms, including:

❖ Leaders who just can't say "no" or stay focused.

❖ Leaders who have the capacity to focus, but when faced with difficult, skill-testing tasks or more work than time will allow, routinely choose to do that which is easiest rather than most important.

- ❖ Leaders who do not prioritize. They spend excessive time, attention, and resources on activities that are not in the critical path of achieving significant goals.

- ❖ Leaders who are still pursuing an idea or project that is no longer viable. These are leaders who are too attached to what could have happened but is not going to happen. These leaders "keep on keeping on" anyway.

These are stark descriptions of *Being Distracted*. There are many subtle variations that most of us can easily relate to. Just one of those is Ginny's story at the beginning of the chapter:

Ginny is a senior leader, and her colleagues and direct reports rely on her clarity and guidance. However, Ginny is not keeping up. She spends hours and hours on email, and she finds it increasingly difficult to stay on top of the many meetings and staff demands that are placed upon her.

This initial description gives us a glimpse into just one of the demands on Ginny's time. Her lack of efficiency with her email is our concern, not the fact that she attends to it at all. The issue is her willingness to be distracted by reading and responding to all of her email in real time, whether or not it is required. The result is that Ginny is not organized, and she is not attending to what matters most.

The Cost of Being Distracted

It's easy to see the consequences of *Being Distracted* when it is excessive:

❖ Reduced productivity

❖ Loss of collegial respect

❖ Attending to minor problems and opportunities

❖ Inadvertently creating new, potentially more serious, problems elsewhere

Each of these costs has significant ramifications that can affect us personally and professionally. Reduced productivity is clearly harmful to our organizations and as leaders, we are also negatively influencing those we are supervising and mentoring. If our peers and colleagues lose respect for us, we are less influential; the costs of wielding less sway are considerable when important decisions must be made. When we attend to less rather than more significant problems because they are "easier," we leave the bigger issues unattended. At the very least, those larger issues remain unaddressed, and just as frequently, they evolve into more serious and complex problems.

SEDUCTION 5 *No!*

Is "no" always a poor response? Absolutely not. *No!* is not about objecting when our concerns are well-founded. Nor is it about making and implementing decisions that are difficult but necessary. It is not even about having the occasional sour attitude. This Seduction is about being in a *constant* state of resistance. The emphasis in this

Seduction is on the word "constant." It is closely akin to *Checking Out*. But the difference is that while *Checking Out* comes in many forms, *No!* comes in only one form: No!

This Seduction is about being stuck in a bad mood on most days, if not every day. It is about finding fault with many or all aspects of our work environments repeatedly. This is the Seduction that predisposes us to being like Mikey in the seminal Life cereal commercial: "Give it to Mikey. He won't eat it; he hates everything."

Unfortunately, we all know people like Mikey. The invitation now is to ask yourself whether you are one of them and, if you are, to consider whether this is a Seduction you choose to continue.

Like all Seductions, *No!* also comes in variations and even disguised forms. Some of these are:

- ❖ Feeling or appearing confused and saying "I don't know" a lot

- ❖ Challenging most initiatives with "It won't work"

- ❖ Withholding information and opinions even when they are called for (which can look like *Checking Out* and which may be a combination of *Checking Out* and resisting)

- ❖ Being quiet or supporting something or someone in meetings and then sabotaging or speaking negatively about those same people or initiatives afterward

- ❖ Attempting to enroll others in a decidedly negative point of view

Monique's story at the beginning of the chapter is a real-life example of this Seduction:

Monique appears to be in a perpetually negative frame of mind. She is a manager on a complex unit with three other managers, and whenever they brainstorm ways to improve their services and address their area's deficiencies, she shoots down every idea.

The shorthand way for you to tell if you are succumbing to *No!* is to monitor the number of times you exhibit these behaviors and resist change. Note that the Seduction is not in the resistance itself; it is in its frequency. You and most leaders have the obligation to say no when it is your job and you are providing your opinion about an issue that is your responsibility.

Chances are that if you find yourself frequently fighting people, changes in procedures, ways of operating, or other key aspects of your work, it is because you are stuck in *No!*. The point here is to notice that you have fallen into the enticing place of resisting as a habit. Instead of letting that become a way of life, valiant leaders will catch themselves in the act, work to understand why they are battling so much, and decide what they want to do about it."

The Cost of No!

Here again, we see the enormous costs of Seductions that go unattended. We could examine a short list of these costs, but this Seduction deserves a thorough look at the biggest cost of all. It is difficult to lead valiantly when our behaviors turn others away. Extremely negative leaders have a seriously debilitating effect on those around them. Colleagues, peers, direct reports, and co-workers will have reactions ranging from staying away from these leaders to leaving them altogether. They may also withhold good ideas and information because they don't want to hear the naysayer's responses. Worse, some colleagues may be overcome and "infected" by such negative leaders and eventually they, too, will join the cause of resistance.

Unfortunately, there are managers and leaders who see but do not address these negative people, because they do not have the skills or the fortitude to do so. Such insightful but reluctant observers can't find a way to lean into their own Leadership Valor, even when their organization and other staff are being affected in significant ways.

> *"Unfortunately, there are managers and leaders who see but do not address negative people, because they do not have the skills or the fortitude to do so."*

SEDUCTION 6 *It's All About You*

Like all Seductions, *It's All About You* has many faces and forms. Here are some of them:

- ❖ "I didn't do it; they did."
- ❖ "I'm fine, but you're not."

❖ "You (or they) need help, need to change, are not listening, did the wrong thing, aren't prepared, etc." This version is based on an internal dialogue that goes something like this: "I've taken your inventory, and I know that you are deficient in these ways."

❖ "You are (or he is or she is) more prepared, more important or 'better' than I am."

You're probably beginning to have a good understanding of this Seduction with only these few clues. The key to this Seduction is that we are overly focused on other people. To indulge in this Seduction is to abandon an appropriate amount of focus and attention on ourselves.

From time to time, leaders may compare themselves to others and feel that they are superior or deficient. However, these occasional indulgences do not meet the requirement of being Seductions because they are relatively short-lived or infrequent.

Louise's story at the beginning of the chapter illustrates *It's All About You*:

Louise is very annoyed with her boss and his explanations about why he cannot give her the additional resources she needs. In passing, she has requested more staff support several times. She can't stop thinking about how ill-prepared he is for his position, and she fantasizes about telling his boss about his failings.

The key in this Seduction is not that Louise disagrees with her boss; it is that she is blaming him rather than considering what role she has in this problem. Notice that she has asked her boss for more staff "in passing." If she has only asked for additional support in passing, it is entirely possible that Louise has not presented a solid business case that her boss can approve.

As the last bullet point in the list at the beginning of this section illustrates, there are still other forms of *It's All About You*. For example, let's say a leader, Beverly, is fixated on a new co-worker, Ayesha, who has just joined the team. Ayesha has a strong reputation and stellar credentials. Beverly watches Ayesha's every move and studies her in meetings. She becomes very concerned that Ayesha is "better" than she is. In this case, this Seduction may also look like *Checking Out* because Beverly is concentrating on distractions and/or *Storytelling*. However we characterize it, Beverly is disproportionately focused on Ayesha, and she is concocting stories about how great Ayesha is. The Seduction is that she is concentrating on a co-worker instead of herself, and she is doing it excessively.

When focusing on the other is so overdone that the other leader's stature becomes too important, we are witnessing *It's All About You*. Notice that this scenario is not the same as a leader who is watching another as a role model or mentor; that could be a valiant leader in the making.

The Cost of It's All About You

There are two important consequences of an exaggerated focus on "the other":

❖ Leaders whose concentration is stuck on the qualities and actions of other people may not be taking responsibility for their own actions and impact. Louise's story is a good example. She is so fixated on her boss and all his shortcomings that she has yet to consider her own role in the situation. While she fantasizes about telling her boss's manager about his "issues," it is highly likely that Louise is already sharing those thoughts with her peers. Louise's unwillingness to look at her own part in this disagreement could be costly to her boss's reputation, and it will almost certainly be costly to Louise's reputation, too.

❖ Co-workers notice *It's All About You* behavior, particularly when it goes unchecked by the organization. No one wants to work in unpleasant organizational cultures in which blaming flourishes. Who knows how many people are disaffected, leave, or do not apply to work in these organizations in the first place.

SEDUCTIONS AND THE JOURNEY OF LEADERSHIP VALOR

The purpose of learning about the Seductions is to shed light on temptations that are natural and human. Recognizing them is part of the experience of being a valiant leader. Knowing about these Six Leadership Seductions will not expunge them from your work or personal life. That would be an unattainable goal. Your goal is not to punish yourself if and when you find yourself steeped in—or about to be steeped in—a Seduction. Instead, the goal is to notice what is happening and to decide what to do about it as you travel the courageous yet imperfect road to strong, potent, valiant leadership.

The value of understanding whether and how the Seductions are relevant for you is that you can recognize them when they show up. The difference between knowing and not knowing about them is that when you know, you can catch yourself and make a deliberate choice. You can choose to stop the Seduction from amplifying and taking over your experience. Or, you can go along with the Seduction because you are simply not ready to do otherwise. Even if you do go along for a while, now that you know about Seductions, it is likely that sooner rather than later, you will make a different choice. You will elect to be lead valiantly, and that is what we explore in the next chapter.

> ## BEING VALIANT
>
> "The value of understanding whether and how the Seductions are relevant for you is that you can recognize them when they show up. The difference between knowing and not knowing about the Seductions is that when you know, you can catch yourself and make a deliberate choice."

KEY TAKE-AWAYS

❖ A Leadership Seduction is a powerful "hook," usually an unconscious temptation, habit, or operating strategy."

❖ Almost all leaders engage in at least mild versions of one or more of these patterns on occasion. They are natural human tendencies that may comfort us even though they are not sustainable solutions to the serious requirements of leading healthcare now.

❖ An attitude or behavior becomes a Seduction when it is long-lasting, intense, and very difficult for a leader to shake. This is distinctly different from using the same coping strategy for a brief period and in a much diluted form.

❖ Leading with valor does not mean you are Seduction-free. That would be an unattainable goal. Instead, the goal is to notice what is happening and to choose to continue the behavior of the Seduction or not.

❖ Knowing about and understanding the power of Leadership Seductions will not give you immunity to them. However, the knowledge you gained in this chapter will equip you so you will recognize them when they occur. You now know what the Seductions can do, not only to you but also to those around you.

3

THE FOUR STEPS
OF LEADERSHIP
VALOR

Now that you know about the Six Leadership Seductions and how they can affect your capacity to lead valiantly, we are ready to explore the Four Steps of Leadership Valor. Jackie's journey, as captured in the following story, will anchor the introduction of each step so you can see the entire process unfold.

Jackie was a senior leader in a regional healthcare organization. She was fairly new in her role, and she was facing a significant professional predicament. She didn't feel content in her job, despite her careful deliberation when taking this position less than a year ago. We meet Jackie when she was being heavily recruited to go elsewhere; she was also at odds with several peers. She had demanding, important work to do, and the financial realities of her organization required her immediate attention. Yet she was finding it difficult to concentrate and just get the job done.

We encounter Jackie when she was faced with a choice. She was in high demand, and she could make a job change with relative ease. But she did not want to go in that direction without giving her circumstances a lot of thought. So, Jackie chose to follow a specific process of considered reflection instead.

Jackie, like many leaders, was accustomed to putting out fires every day. She, like many leaders, knew that effective stewardship requires prompt and best-effort responses to multiple demands and circumstances. Jackie was adept at quickly resolving most situations she encountered. So, she often reacted immediately, and this approach was usually effective. Jackie's typical way of responding demonstrates the "mini-loop of expediency," as depicted in Figure 3.1.

Resolution   **Situation**

FIGURE 3.1   THE MINI-LOOP OF EXPEDIENCY

THE CYCLE OF LEADERSHIP VALOR

What was different about Jackie's dilemma, however, was that the stakes were high and there was not a ready answer that felt right. While it was tempting to simply solve her problem by taking a well-paying position elsewhere, Jackie knew she might regret this quick and easy solution, no matter how attractive a new job sounded. She did not want to just react, nor did she want to act without thinking about the long-term consequences and the Leadership Seductions that might be influencing her. Instead, she wanted to think carefully about herself at this stage of her career and her life.

It was important to Jackie to make the important choices before her with care and mindfulness. So, instead of opting for an expedient resolution (the mini-loop), she decided to move through the Cycle of Leadership Valor. The Cycle of Leadership Valor is made up of the four steps shown in Figure 3.2 on the next page.

In this chapter, you will learn about the steps in the Cycle, as well as the underlying concepts that serve as their foundation. As you read, you will find Guideposts—exercises and other reflective opportunities—to help you consider the steps and how they relate to your own opportunities and challenges.

Before you begin reading, know that you don't have to have a question as big as Jackie's to engage in the Cycle of Leadership Valor. It can be a go-to strategy for small challenges and opportunities, and you can also use it for strategic or potentially career-altering choices. Each time you access the Cycle, you can decide how much or how little time you want to devote to a given step. Over time, as you'll discover in Chapter 5, you'll find easy ways to remember the steps, and you'll learn to adjust and use them to suit you and your circumstances. No matter how you approach the steps, you will find that each turn of the Cycle adds to your capacity to lead valiantly.

FIGURE 3.2   THE CYCLE OF LEADERSHIP VALOR

The steps are arrayed as a spiral to convey that:

❖ The requirements of leadership are constantly evolving.

❖ As valiant leaders, we are continually learning in order to meet the demands and opportunities inherent in the world of healthcare.

Each step in the Cycle of Leadership Valor is described in detail in the following sections.

STEP 1   *Initiate*

The Cycle of Leadership Valor starts when you choose self-awareness rather than a response that is automatic and routine. As Jackie's story demonstrates, *Initiate* invites you to take a different journey—a journey that begins with stepping back to pause and to consider rather than to react. Just taking this first step can be difficult, particularly when circumstances are complex and decisions must be made quickly.

By *Initiating*, Jackie is electing to enhance her self-awareness. In making this choice, she is deepening what the Center for Creative Leadership (CCL) described as a "meta-competency" in its 2011 report on leadership development best practices (Petrie, 2011). Precisely because of most leaders' bias toward action, the first step supports this increasingly important leadership capability.

What's important about this first step is that you as a leader always have a choice. No matter what pressures you are experiencing, unless they are true emergencies, you can *Initiate* and reflect.

BEING VALIANT

"No matter what pressures you are experiencing, unless they are true emergencies, you can *Initiate* and reflect."

As you enhance your own way of leading valiantly, the value of bypassing the ever-tempting mini-loop of expediency will become apparent. Once you *Initiate*, you will gain many benefits from increasing your self-awareness; the Guidepost lists a few of these advantages along with ways to deepen this valuable leadership competency.

YOU, LEADING VALIANTLY

What would prompt you to choose to *Initiate* the Cycle of Leadership Valor? Here are a few examples of circumstances that can prod you to take this first step:

❖ You know that what is at stake is important enough to warrant a thoughtful pause, no matter how urgent a situation appears to be.

❖ You stop yourself if what is demanding your attention is beyond your expertise, experience, or scope of responsibility.

❖ You want to quiet yourself so you can hear your own thoughts.

❖ You need time to become more comfortable with something you are about to do or have already done.

❖ You catch yourself when you are about to react impulsively, and you think your response may not be appropriate.

If a rapid-response approach is automatic for you as a leader, choosing to pause and increase your self-awareness may feel awkward at first. Nonetheless, you will benefit from making this choice when circumstances call for your best.

YOU, LEADING VALIANTLY

Here are some ways to expand your self-awareness:

❖ Give yourself space to simply "be" and think. Simple as this sounds, most leaders deprive themselves of the opportunity to be without structure for even a short period of time. But doing so allows you to tap into wisdom that is simply not available to you when you are hyper-busy.

❖ Pursue the counsel of people you trust.

❖ Seek greater understanding of your skills and perspectives as they relate to the situation you are facing.

❖ Consider the other resources or support you need to successfully manage your opportunity or challenge.

STEP 2 *Illuminate*

The second step in the cycle is *Illuminate.* Here is where Leadership Valor comes to life. This step invites you to update your thinking about who you are, what you want, and, significantly, what can get in the way of achieving it. Don't be concerned about how "big" this sounds. It does not have to be a lengthy and time-consuming exploration. In fact, it can take just a few seconds to remember what is important to you or to pull yourself away from ill-advised action. Or, if you wish, you can spend considerably more time with this step. The choice of how much time you spend and how deep you go in Step 2: *Illuminate* is yours.

In this step you will engage in two distinct explorations. The first is to think more broadly about the circumstances and "reality" you are experiencing. The second is to recognize that Seductions could be influencing you. We begin by taking a fresh look at "reality" and how a larger understanding of the basics of your own life can firmly anchor you in valiant leadership.

Levels of Reality: What They Are and What They Mean to You

Many schools of thought and religious traditions refer to "worlds" and "realities" other than the here and now. What these universal belief systems have in common are their attempts to interpret what we think of as *reality*, or the totality of our life experience. Plato offered one example when he cited the three parts of the human soul: reason, appetite, and spirit (Brown, 2011). These are akin to the Three Levels of Reality that will inform your journey of Leadership Valor: consensus reality, essence reality, and dreaming reality (see Figure 3.3). This tradition was originated by the Australian aborigines and carried forward into modern leadership and organizational thinking by Arnold and Amy Mindell (2012) and by Faith Fuller, PhD and Marita Fridjhon, MSW, of the Center for Right Relationship (Fuller & Fridjhon, 2007).[i]

---

[i] I am very grateful to Faith Fuller and Marita Fridjhon for their graciousness, their work with these three levels, and the ways I have found to apply them to my own leadership models.

FIGURE 3.3   THE THREE LEVELS OF REALITY

As you review the Three Levels of Reality, consider whether you are aware of them in your daily life now. With access to all of them, you can maintain a well-rounded view of your circumstances and your options. In fact, examining multiple perspectives instead of just one is a key facet of mastery, a topic explored further in Chapter 6, "Mastering Valiant Leadership." What is relevant here is that masters of their crafts often develop multiple points of view when they create. For example, Leonardo da Vinci routinely captured his subjects from at least three vantage points, and from these several renderings, he was able to craft his stunning works of art (Gelb, 2000).

Consensus reality. Consensus reality is easy to understand because it includes the "stuff" of your everyday life. It encompasses everything that is concrete, as well as facts, data, and events. This is the physical world and all its material representations. You can measure most aspects of consensus reality: They are tangible and solid. We work with consensus reality in each waking moment as we navigate our physical environment.

Note that "consensus reality" is not the same as "consensus decision-making." Also note that there are myriad examples of consensus reality. Just a few are the everyday facts in Jackie's story. For example, most of the opening statements are facts about Jackie that reflect consensus reality: She is relatively new to her position; she is a senior leader in a healthcare organization; and she has other colleagues. The concerns she has about her co-workers and the compelling nature of her job offers are also part of Jackie's consensus reality. So, too, are her organization's financial constraints.

YOU, LEADING VALIANTLY

Take a moment to consider the importance of consensus reality in healthcare organizations. Also consider whether leaders are inspiring when they communicate from *only* the perspective that consensus reality provides. That means that *all* they talk about are facts, metrics, and tangible goals.

Do you believe that leaders inspire when this reality is the whole of their message? Probably not. As critically important as the facts are, much of the healthcare workforce is enlivened and motivated when leaders speak about more than just data, problems, and measures.

Jackie offers a good example of the important yet limiting aspects of concentrating entirely on this one dimension of reality. While she was keenly aware of the work she needed to do, she also knew that she was missing something. She was uncomfortable with her circumstances, but she was not ready to make a decision. She needed to think about more than the facts that were immediately in front of her. That's why Jackie decided to pause. She knew that revealing other equally valuable perspectives would inform her choices for the future.

YOU, LEADING VALIANTLY

1. Identify a few opportunities or challenges you are facing on the job.

2. Consider each opportunity or challenge carefully and then select one that is particularly important to you. Take a few minutes to define your issue:

   ❖ What is the opportunity or problem?

   ❖ Why is it important to you?

   ❖ What is its current status?

   Notice that you are probably describing aspects of consensus reality as you do this.

3. Consider how you feel about this opportunity or challenge:

   ❖ Are you eager to tackle it?

   ❖ Whether you are or aren't, ask yourself if you could use more inspiration, more motivation, and perhaps more courage. If so, you will benefit from knowing about the other two Levels of Reality.

Essence reality. The next level of reality is *essence reality*, or the sentient level of what is "real." Sentient and essence are synonymous; they both reflect the living spirit of something. Essence is the very nature of that something. It is also the very nature of a person. It is the answer we give ourselves when we ask questions such as "Who am I?" or "What is most important to me?" As noted earlier in this chapter, answering these essential questions can be a lengthy exploration, but it doesn't have to be. It can also be a simple "check-in."

"Sentient and essence are synonymous; they both reflect the living spirit of something."

Essence is difficult to describe completely, but we "know it when we see it." Integrity is a good example of essence: We know leaders with integrity when we see them. While most descriptions like "honest" and "congruent" are accurate enough, they don't capture the whole of those leaders' integrity.

Essence can also be defined as what is most vital or important about a person, a company, a healthcare organization, or a culture. A good organizational example of essence is Apple, Inc., the global technology company. As you read the word "Apple," perhaps you thought about a descriptor of Apple within seconds of seeing its name. Perhaps you envisioned its iconic "Apple" logo. This reaction happens for people who know this company because Apple stands for something, be it innovation, design, utility, or customer loyalty. But which of those descriptions "is" Apple? We could say all of them "are" Apple; yet we also know that none of them "is" Apple.

We have trouble with this exercise because we are trying to clearly capture and define the essence of Apple. That task is nearly impossible, yet most of us understand the essence of Apple because "we know it when we see it."

Before this exploration gets too far removed from you as a leader, let's rejoin Jackie so you can see how this concept applies to you and your journey of valiant leadership.

Jackie decided to go for a walk as she considered her own essence. She thought about how to respond to questions like "Who am I, really, at this stage of my life?" Although she could have given pat responses like "I am a mother, wife, healthcare professional, etc.," she wanted to go beyond just naming her roles in life. But when she left the roles behind, she found she did not have ready answers. Still, she didn't get discouraged; instead she took her time as she answered the questions in the next Guidepost.

YOU, LEADING VALIANTLY

1. Find a comfortable spot. Take a journal if you like.

2. Once you are settled, write or think about what comes to your mind when you reflect on who you are at this juncture of your leadership career. Also reflect on what you stand for and what is most important to you. Notice whatever shows up; if you have no answers for one of the questions, move on to the next. There is no right way to do this exercise, and there are no wrong answers. Here are some ways to begin:

   ❖ Imagine how a family member or good friend would describe you and what is really important to you.

❖ Think about your values, faith, and times that give you great joy, and times you feel relaxed and refreshed.

❖ What symbols represent who you are and what is most important to you?

❖ Remember yourself as a child. What were you like then? What was important to you? How do these qualities and values affect you now?

No matter how you engage with these questions, let your imagination go.

3. When you are finished, reflect on your own answers.

❖ What do your thoughts reveal about you now, at this moment and at this stage of your life and your career?

❖ What is significant about your discoveries?

4. Think carefully about these next questions:

❖ How can you bring the wisdom of these reflections into your life as a valiant leader?

❖ What bearing do they have on your problem or opportunity?

The goal of this exercise is not to nail down what your essence is. It is to give you time to acknowledge and relax into this level of your being. It is also to identify the essential qualities that describe you and to *Illuminate* parts of yourself that will give you courage and direction.

As Jackie worked through this same exercise, she reached a deeper understanding of herself, particularly when she thought about the benefits that exercise gave her. Her morning workout routines left her feeling centered and free of distraction. She thought about how true-to-herself she felt after working out because she had settled into a state of calm, clear, personal power. In those moments, she had a vivid sense of her values and what "doing the right thing" meant to her. She left her workouts with strength and clarity that she carried into her work life. Throughout the rest of the day, she stayed focused, productive, and even somewhat "light."

Dreaming reality. The third level of reality is *dreaming*, and it is as important as the other realities. It is about our aspirations, and while it is not measurable, it, too, has a profound impact on us. The dreaming level of reality includes our emotions, fantasies, deeply held goals, and even daydreams. It is about possibility and creativity; it contains wisdom, and it is the force that inspires and pulls us forward as human beings. It also represents our aims for the future and contains our deepest wishes to achieve and to serve.

YOU, LEADING VALIANTLY

1. Find your comfortable spot again and write in your journal if you like.

2. From the questions below, choose those that most resonate with you. See where your mind and heart take you as you respond. Even if you are pressed for time, try to resist the temptation to answer automatically. Instead, be open to the questions and answer from the core of who you are. Consider what is true for you *now*.

   ❖ What would you most like to accomplish in this world?

   ❖ What inspires you?

   ❖ What makes you truly happy?

   ❖ Where would you most like to focus your attention?

   ❖ Is there an object or a treasure that is meaningful to you, perhaps even sacred, that represents your dreams?

   ❖ What qualities describe you when you are at your best?

   ❖ What is different about you when you are at your best?

   ❖ What about your leadership would be different if you were at your best more often?

   ❖ What outcomes could you expect if you were your best as a leader more frequently?

These and similar questions can reveal you to you. You may tap into a version of yourself that you are acutely familiar with and that serves as your foundation every day. It's equally possible that you will have an entirely new perspective.

Let's go back to Jackie as she contemplated her dreams and aspirations:

> *Jackie reflected on her wishes and dreams now, not her dreams from the past. This was an important shift for her. Her two children had recently left for college; for many years her ambitions had been about helping her kids launch their lives by giving them great educations. But their "nest leaving" was a significant transition for Jackie, so it was time to update what she most wanted. As soon as she shifted her thinking, her new dream became clear: She wanted to start her own business.*

The Importance of the Three Levels of Reality

How we understand and honor the Three Levels of Reality is important for a number of reasons. The first is that each of us has a natural tendency to favor one of these perspectives. Expressing this preference can have an inordinate influence on what we emphasize when we make decisions and lead others, as we will explore in Chapter 5.

Additionally, to truly excel as a healthcare steward, you and all of us must operate with full-fledged integrity and motivation. We don't need to simply react when compelling circumstances require so much of us.

Instead, when you want to lead valiantly, you can choose to acknowledge your Three Levels of Reality and let them balance
and ground you in the whole of who you are. You can engage in
the tough work of leadership from a solid foundation of what is
meaningful and important to you. You will have an underpinning
of courage and real integrity; both are palpable leadership qualities
that can fulfill, strengthen, and sustain you like no others.

BEING VALIANT

"When you want to lead valiantly, you can choose to acknowledge
your Three Levels of Reality and let them balance and ground you in
the whole of who you are."

Recognizing Seductions

The second part of *Illuminate* focuses on the Six Leadership Seductions, and it offers you the chance to consider whether one or more
of these behaviors, attitudes, and feelings covered in Chapter 2 has
you in its grip:

1. *I Am Right*
2. *Storytelling*
3. *Checking Out*
4. *Being Distracted*
5. *No!*
6. *It's All About You*

Powerful as the questions about your Three Levels of Reality are,
your answers will not always reveal all that is going on for you.

That's why it's important to recognize whether the Seductions are influencing you. If you're not sure, you can refer to "How Do You Know If You Are Experiencing a Leadership Seduction?" on page 31 in Chapter 2 to check.

If you find that you are ensnared in one or more of the Seductions, think about their consequences and whether you want to let it—or them—go. Acknowledging that you are engaged with the Seductions takes courage all by itself; letting go of the Seductions can take even more fortitude. Whether you choose to release them or not, know that neither choice is "bad" or "wrong." What matters is that you know where you stand and that you consciously decide what to do. Leading valiantly is not about being perfect. It is about making conscious choices and being aware of the consequences. When we lead valiantly, we are awake to our Seductions, and we deliberately manage them.

"When we lead valiantly, we are awake to our Seductions, and we deliberately manage them."

Here's what happened for Jackie as she continued the work of the second step, *Illuminate*:

Jackie was pleased with what she uncovered about who she was at that stage of her life and what she really wanted in her career. As she thought about her work, her skills, her age, and the many opportunities that lay before her, she started to feel more alive than she had in months. She knew that launching a business was risky and that it would take a lot of careful planning. But the prospect of having her own healthcare firm really excited her. However, there was something that felt unfinished, and it was holding her back. She was still not clear about what to do with her challenges in her current job.

She moved on to the second part of Illuminate. *She wanted to think about the Seductions and whether they were affecting her work. It didn't take her long to realize that she was stuck in a form of* I Am Right *and* It's All About You. *She didn't like it, but she admitted that her version of* I Am Right *was that she was flattered by the wonderful job offers and the constant reinforcement of how "fabulous" she was. She also saw herself clearly in* It's All About You *because she had built up a near-fixation about the many wrongdoings of her fellow team members. Although she was not happy when she realized that she had fallen into these Seductions, she was relieved to understand what was happening.*

But relief was not enough; Jackie had decisions to make. Just because she recognized the Seductions did not mean she was going to let them go. It was easy enough to release the temporary sense of self-importance the job offers gave her. But she wasn't sure she was ready to let go of her problems with her peers. Nor was she certain about what she wanted "moving on" to look like in the short run. So, Jackie decided she needed a little time to absorb the knowledge and feelings she had uncovered so she could eventually take the next step in the Cycle of Leadership Valor.

STEP 3 *Curate*

We leave Jackie in a contemplative state at the end of *Illuminate*, but she knows she must soon be ready to act. Jackie is preparing for Step 3: *Curate*. This step is about putting it all together and moving ahead.

Why use the word "curate" rather than simply "plan and implement"? The term *curator* is fitting for valiant leadership because it connotes expertise, polish, responsibility, discernment, and the ability to prioritize and to monitor. The word "curator" is derived from the Latin words "curatus" and "accurare." Accurare means "to expend care on" or "to take care of" (Robertson, n.d.). A synonym for curator is "custodian" or "a guardian or keeper, as of an art collection" (Custodian, n.d.). The relevance to us is that a curator is like a guardian or content specialist invested with the care of something important, be it art treasures or furnishings in a home or place of business.

Here is the important point: When it comes to Leadership Valor, you are the guardian of yourself and your leadership. This is not to suggest a grand, time-consuming version of self-focus and self-care that, most likely, you will not sustain. *Curating* simply means that you are aware of the many facets of who you are as a leader. When you embrace that you are the curator of your own leadership, you are consciously entrusting yourself with envisioning, implementing, and then adjusting your actions going forward.

"You are the guardian of yourself and your leadership."

The key to this step, like Step 1: *Initiate*, is that you have a choice. In this third step, you—as curator—actively select the leadership qualities and skills that are most important and relevant to you now. You first choose to create your plan, and then you choose how to implement and calibrate your approach.

Create Your Plan

We see the first part of *Curate* come to life by observing Jackie as she moved out of *Illuminate* and strategized how she was going to proceed.

> *Jackie had learned a lot about herself. She had gotten in touch with her new dream of having her own business, and she recognized the Seductions that were holding her back. It wasn't long before she was ready to give most of her colleagues a second chance by being more open to their opinions. She was prepared to release those Seductions and move into action. She thoughtfully considered her strategy. She soon became clear that she wanted to "grab the bull by the horns" and do the job for which she was hired, at least for a time. While she wasn't sure how long she'd stay, she decided that as long as she remained in her role, she would do what was required to meet the organization's goals.*
>
> *Jackie said that making this decision and creating her plan felt "great." It freed her energy and allowed her to focus on what was important. She considered herself to be an ethical leader, and she wanted to do the right thing. She was ready and eager to get back to work.*

Calibrate Your Approach

Every leader knows that preparation and planning are important but not enough to guarantee exemplary results. No matter how exceptional our plans, we are rarely able to implement them exactly as we imagined. That is why *Curate* includes not only making and implementing plans, but also calibrating those plans and our actions as needed.

Calibrate in this context means the willingness to bend and to be receptive. It is an invitation to thoughtfully adjust. As you move into executing your plans, you will have a different and deeper sensibility about yourself. You will also see the importance of the different perspectives that you may develop and that others may offer. It is not that new perspectives are "right" and your original plan was "wrong"; it is that different inputs may inform your original choices in important ways—ways you will or will not choose to incorporate in your strategies as you go forward. You may see new information or perspectives as irrelevant, or interesting but not important, or you may see that they invite more possibilities and deserve consideration. As noted earlier in this chapter, Leonardo Da Vinci frequently made several versions of his pieces before he combined the best into his final compositions. You, too, have the choice to develop other perspectives and alter your plans and your actions.

This step highlights flexibility, learning-as-you-go, and adjusting so you can reach your goal. It also describes what happens in real life. Think about how airplanes fly. Pilots rarely (perhaps never) leave their originating cities and land at their destinations without subtle and sometimes major shifts in the air.

AN EXAMPLE OF CALIBRATION FROM THE WORLD OF PHOTOGRAPHY

Dewitt Jones is a renowned *National Geographic* photographer. In his video *Everyday Creativity,* Jones (1999) talks about his use of different camera filters and lenses when he takes his photographs. As his experience of a scene deepens, or when the environment around him shifts, he elects to use different pieces of equipment so he can capture the image that is most compelling.

As a masterful artist, he is making a conscious choice to change perspectives so he is not stuck with a single, mediocre, or undesirable result. As masterful and valiant leaders, we can calibrate, too. We do not need to stick with positions or statements that will not lead to the outcomes we seek.

In your own leadership life, you are the pilot, or curator, and you already shift and accommodate, too—sometimes a little and sometimes a lot. The core of this step is about planning with a deeper appreciation of who you are and adjusting your leadership when and if you so choose.

Does it take courage to adjust and change positions publicly? Yes. It takes valor. You don't have to develop a plan and stick to it, no matter what. You can choose to correct mid-course, even if it is not what others want or expect.

"You don't have to develop a plan and stick to it, no matter what. You can choose to correct mid-course, even if it is not what others want or expect."

 YOU, LEADING VALIANTLY

1. In a comfortable position, think (or journal) about an important leadership challenge you recently encountered and successfully managed.

2. Remember how you dealt with that challenge.

3. Consider whether and how you altered your course from the initial development of your plan through the time you started to respond to the time the situation was resolved.

   Did you alter your course?

   ❖ If not, why didn't you, and what was the benefit of that strategy?

   ❖ If you did shift while pursuing your goal, what caused you to shift, and what was the benefit of adjusting?

We return to Jackie as she executes her plan and experiences an opportunity to calibrate her approach.

Jackie was ready and eager to jump back into the fray. Over the next few weeks, she devised and implemented financial strategies to achieve the budget reductions that were sorely needed in her organization. She had difficult but imperative conversations with direct reports who were affected by these reductions.

She was about to wrap up the last of these dialogues when the team member she was speaking with, Colin, asked for additional time. She had told Colin that he would be losing a member of his staff so she was more than willing to listen. In the subsequent dialogue, Colin did talk about the impact of losing his staff member. As the conversation evolved, however, he also told Jackie that the team that reported to her admired her, but also somewhat feared her. Although this really surprised Jackie, she respected Colin's willingness to give her this feedback. She told him she appreciated his courage, and she asked him to tell her more so she could fully understand. She assured him that he would be safe and that she would not hold his statements against him. Colin obliged, and by the end of their meeting, Jackie had a new perspective on how she was perceived by some of those who worked for her.

Had Jackie been unwilling or unable to hear any viewpoint other than her own, she would have missed this critical feedback. But Jackie was open and deeply grateful for Colin's own valiant leadership, and she took his message to heart. She was also convinced that she needed to change how she dealt with some of her staff members. She left work that day filled with questions and initial ideas about what she was going to do differently.

YOU, LEADING VALIANTLY

1. Think about the opportunity or challenge you identified in Step 2: *Illuminate* (see the Guidepost on page 67).

2. Remember what you learned about yourself in that step and consider how your Three Levels of Reality and possible Seductions will impact how you can best deal with this issue.

3. Think about how you want to put it all together and *Curate* your leadership to address your situation valiantly. Putting it all together and curating invites you to ask yourself these kinds of questions:

   ❖ What skills and perspectives will help you manage this situation most effectively?

   ❖ Are there skills, perspectives, or attitudes that you want to de-emphasize?

   ❖ What does your plan look like?

   ❖ How and when will you implement it?

   ❖ Do you have what you need to go forward?

   ❖ If not, what else do you need, and how are you going to meet those needs?

   ❖ What circumstances may prompt you to calibrate and adjust your strategy? Are you willing to shift if you need to?

4. When you are ready, implement your plan. Celebrate the fact that you have positioned yourself to be successful. Remember that regardless of the outcome, you are practicing valiant leadership.

RESOLUTION

Jackie's story to this point leaves us with an understanding of three of the four steps. She has more to do, but as she leaves *Curate*, Jackie has reached a "resolution" to the situation that initially prompted her to take this journey. She embraced her future direction, she recommitted to her job, she trimmed the budget, she had needed conversations, and she knew her team respected her, even in these tough times. At the same time, Jackie learned that she needed to change how she was communicating with some of her staff members. She knew this because she was open to hearing a different perspective, even when it included critical feedback.

This resolution was satisfying to Jackie. Still, like many resolutions, it also brought more challenges. This stable but temporary state is like much of leadership life. We often "resolve" one challenge and, when we're done, we are faced with a new challenge, perhaps stemming from a previous decision or success.

How Much Resolution Is Enough?

Leading with valor does not require that the original situation be resolved completely. The question to ask is: How much progress is enough, for now?

Part of skilled calibration is your willingness to discern what level of resolution is acceptable. Pilots practice this kind of discernment, too. They shift a little or a lot, to keep moving. Together, these small or great individual modifications become the whole of the path that guides them to their ultimate destination. Their flight plan is a series of steps, alterations, and accommodations. So, too, is your journey toward valiant leadership.

STEP 4 *Integrate*

Every leader is familiar with the press of too much to do and not enough time to do it. The Cycle of Leadership Valor honors that reality while also including a step that self-aware leaders don't ignore. It is the deliberate process of integration. Step 4: *Integrate* recognizes the value of internalizing what you have learned. This step is less about a specified amount of time or a particular place to reflect and more about an intention to learn.

You can complete this step in whatever way works best for you. What is important is your commitment to your own growth. *Integrate* is about remembering the insights and wisdom you gained from leading valiantly as you did the work of the previous three steps. Without Step 4: *Integrate,* at least some of your learning will be lost.

"Integrate is about remembering the insights and wisdom you gained from leading valiantly as you did the work of the previous three steps."

Integrate encourages you to assimilate your learning so you can take it forward into your future opportunities. The biggest benefit of incorporating what you have gained is that you will have more capacity to sustain valiant leadership. Jackie's story illustrates one way to "integrate" what she has achieved and learned so far on her journey through the steps.

Jackie thought about all that she had accomplished and what was ahead. Had Jackie been unwilling or unable to hear any viewpoint other than her own, she would have missed this critical feedback. But Jackie was open and deeply grateful for Colin's own valiant leadership, and she took his message to heart.

Jackie had learned that she needed to strengthen her relationships with some of her staff members. She also considered what she had accomplished:

> ❖ *She resolved the situation that initially troubled her.*
>
> ❖ *She got in touch with a deeper sense of herself and her aspirations—not those from the past, but those that were true for her now.*
>
> ❖ *She regained her energy.*
>
> ❖ *She anchored herself in her own power as a leader.*

YOU, LEADING VALIANTLY

1. Find a comfortable spot. Whether you write in a journal or just think, consider the journey you just took.

2. Reflect on what you learned as you worked through the steps, created and calibrated your plan, addressed your opportunity or challenge, and eventually arrived at a permanent or "good-enough" resolution.

   ❖ What wisdom did you gain from the whole experience?

   ❖ What did you do that worked well?

   ❖ What will you do differently next time?

WHERE THE STEPS TAKE YOU

As you have seen, you can enhance your skill as a valiant leader by engaging in the steps in the Cycle of Leadership Valor. Table 3.1 compares leading valiantly with leading without valor.

TABLE 3.1   LEADING WITH AND WITHOUT VALOR

Step on the Path	Leading Without Valor	Leading With Valor
Step 1: *Initiate* Choose Self-Awareness	Reacting, perhaps impulsively, to a compelling situation.	Remembering that you can choose to expand your self-awareness and consciously decide how you will respond.
Step 2: *Illuminate* Reveal Your Three Levels of Reality	Focusing on the facts in the here-and-now, and forgetting, dismissing, or being unaware of the importance of *essence* and aspirations.	Uncovering, remembering, and honoring your *essence* and *dreams*, as well as your *consensus* reality. Bringing all three realities to bear as you fortify your full-bodied, valiant leadership. Remembering that others are inspired by essence and aspirations in addition to the facts of consensus reality.
Step 2: *Illuminate* Recognize Seductions	Not seeing that you are engaged in behaviors and attitudes that sabotage your effectiveness and your results.	Recognizing the Seductions that may be influencing how you are dealing with your circumstances. Either letting go of those Seductions or being aware that you are choosing to hold onto them.

Step on the Path	Leading Without Valor	Leading With Valor
Step 3: *Curate* Create Your Plan	Simply reacting without first grounding yourself in the fullest and most valiant version of your personal power, and creating a plan that is firmly anchored in those qualities.	Putting all the facets of your renewed self-awareness together. Creating a plan that is based on a conscious and balanced view of your essence, your aspirations, your Seductions (if any), and what is happening around you, including the organization's needs and other people's concerns.
Step 3: *Curate* Calibrate Your Approach	Being unwilling to adapt your strategy to changing conditions, new information, or other insights you gather along the way.	Considering whether and/or how you want to adjust your plan as you implement it.
Step 4: *Integrate* Integrate Your Wisdom	Neglecting to reflect on the whole of your experience so you can learn and take your wisdom forward.	Either right away or after some time has passed, reviewing what happened and what you did. Identifying what you learned, what worked, what was less suc-cessful, and what you will do differently next time.

As we conclude our exploration of Leadership Valor and its four steps, we can see how Jackie completed her journey:

At home in the evening, following her meeting with Colin, Jackie felt genuinely excited about being open enough to hear Colin's direct and critical feedback. Although she was concerned about what he said, she was very grateful to him. She was also pleased with herself. Jackie had not always been able to listen to such forthright comments from anyone, let alone someone who reported to her. As she reflected on her day, she was just plain happy that she actually heard what Colin said. It was very important information.

As the evening ended, Jackie knew there was more work to do. She wanted to adjust her communication style with some of her direct reports, and she felt entirely up to the task. Difficult as this might have been just a few days earlier, now Jackie felt enthused and well-equipped to tackle what was ahead. She readied for bed feeling content and fulfilled. She knew she would sleep very well that night.

Jackie's story is an example of using the steps to valiantly address a significant leadership challenge. She opted for greater self-awareness, remembering her essence and her aspirations, uncovering her Seductions, taking action, adjusting her strategy as needed, and integrating her learning. Each move forward through the steps enhanced her journey.

It is easy to imagine that the sum of Jackie's experience will allow her to strengthen and sustain her leadership effectiveness—and valor—for a long time to come. If and when she is challenged again, she will be building on her increased awareness and improved ability to lead with courage, clarity, and integrity.

KEY TAKE-AWAYS

❖ The Cycle of Leadership Valor sets out a deliberate four-step process of reflection and action that supports and sustains you as a valiant leader.

❖ Leaders often opt for the "mini-loop of expediency," in which they react immediately to a situation in order to resolve it quickly. Sometimes, this is appropriate. At other times, however, it short-circuits mindfulness, learning, and optimal results.

❖ The first step, *Initiate*, invites you to choose self-awareness instead of the mini-loop of expediency.

❖ In Step 2: *Illuminate*, you reveal your perspectives on the Three Levels of Reality (consensus, essence, and dreaming) and recognize the Seductions that may be muting your effectiveness.

❖ In Step 3, you *Curate* your leadership by consciously creating a plan of action and calibrating it as needed. You reach a resolution that may be what you set out to achieve, or it may be a different resolution that is acceptable to you.

❖ Step 4: *Integrate* encourages you to reflect and incorporate the learning you gained by going through the other steps. Taking this step prepares you to access the Cycle again with greater wisdom, self-awareness, and clarity.

4

Beyond the Steps: What Else Is Required for Valiant Leadership?

What does it really take to lead with valor? As you read about the steps and the journey that Jackie took in Chapter 3, you may be thinking that valiant leadership is as easy as following the simple recipe contained in the four steps. If that's your impression, the good news is that your assessment is correct. Models, recipes, and easy instructions are enormously valuable for all of us when we learn new skills. We know from Patricia Benner's (1984) seminal work with nursing competencies that "novices" and "advanced beginners" are supported by clear procedures and specific guidelines.

So, whether you are new at leading or an experienced professional, the Cycle and the steps will be useful if leading valiantly is not yet natural for you.

But leaders who are experienced know that potent, spirited stewardship takes more than following a simple progression of steps. While the specific aspects of the Cycle of Leadership Valor are designed to be easy to understand and use, seasoned leaders know that truly courageous leadership takes more. The steps are important because of the insights they will give you, but they cannot capture the rest of what it takes to be a bold, valiant leader on a consistent basis. This chapter explores the remaining ingredients of leading with valor:

❖ The ability to manage both readiness and resistance

❖ The willingness to be bold, to reflect, to unlearn, to be imperfect, and even to fail on occasion

❖ The value of practice

READINESS: THE WILLINGNESS TO LEAD VALIANTLY

What is readiness? Simply stated, readiness is being prepared mentally or physically for an experience or action. It also means being "willingly disposed" and "inclined" (Ready, n.d.). How do you know

know if you are prepared to take the journey of Leadership Valor?
You can say you are ready if you are:

- ❖ Motivated to sharpen your leadership skills

- ❖ Open to trying new approaches

- ❖ Patient about being a little uncomfortable if new strategies
  don't work or seem unnatural at first

- ❖ Willing to reflect, to ask new and potentially thought-
  provoking questions, and to practice

- ❖ Sincerely interested in growing as an individual and as a
  leader

You may see yourself in most or all of these descriptions. It's also
possible that you may not relate to them, but you may still be
drawn to leading valiantly. Or, you may believe you already lead in
this way, yet you want to be more proficient and enjoy more success.

READINESS IS …

Readiness: being prepared mentally or physically for an experience
or action; being "willingly disposed" and "inclined."

YOU, LEADING VALIANTLY

1. Think about whether the descriptions of readiness describe you. If you identify with one or more, you're ready to lead valiantly.

2. If you are not as ready as you could be, what is missing for you?

   ❖ Do you want support from teammates, colleagues, a mentor or supervisor, or a coach?

   ❖ Do you want assurances that your peers or supervisors will approve of you becoming a stronger leader? (Be aware there is no guarantee this will happen.)

   ❖ If everyone is not on board, will you choose to lead valiantly anyway?

In Chapter 3, the Guidepost on page 62 identified several of the circumstances that can serve as motivators to engage the steps of valiant leadership. These circumstances can stem from any of these sources:

1. **What is happening around you.** You may want to be considered for a position that requires a great deal of leadership vision, tenacity, and strength. Or perhaps your current position offers you opportunities to show your leadership mettle in ways you have not shown before. Or maybe your outcomes are not what you want and you want to lead more effectively. It's also conceivable that you have received a serious wakeup call such as being put on notice or worse. These are

examples of externally generated opportunities or problems that are presenting you with the choice to lead differently.

2. **What is happening inside you.** It's possible that there are plenty of leadership demands on you, and you are doing quite well with them. You may be very successful in the here and now. If that's the case, you might want to not only keep it up, but also "step it up." Maybe you want to move ahead in your current job, in your career, and in your life as Jackie demonstrated at the outset of Chapter 3. What is really important now is that you think carefully about what you are doing, how you are doing it, and what you are going to do in the future. Or let's say you simply want to keep in touch with yourself—the fullest version of yourself—so you can lead authentically and with integrity. These are internally generated needs that are prompting you to lead valiantly.

3. **Support from others.** Others can often see potential in leaders when they are not able to see it in themselves. Your peers, mentors, supervisors, or coaches may want you to awaken to your own capacity for leadership excellence.

In short, you can be inspired and ready to take this journey for any number of reasons.

YOU, LEADING VALIANTLY

What Is True for You?

1. What is prompting your interest in expanding your capacity to lead valiantly? Take time to generate as many answers as you have.

2. Recall the vision of yourself as a valiant leader (see the Guidepost on page 23 in Chapter 1).

   ❖ As you turn your vision into reality and you become increasingly valiant, remember that you identified the ways you will be different and the results you want to achieve. What are those differences and results?

   ❖ How will you know you are successful?

RESISTANCE: THE WILLINGNESS TO BE RELUCTANT AND PROCEED ANYWAY

What if you discover you are not ready to lead with valor in a particular circumstance? Does that mean you should relinquish its pursuit entirely? No. It's quite possible that you may experience some resistance to leading bravely on occasion. In fact, it is normal for human beings to resist sometimes, even when our best interests will be served by courageously moving ahead.

Valiant leaders will consciously choose to understand their resistance. As you take the journey of Leadership Valor, your experience will teach you to discern what is going on for you and how your resistance is not serving you or others. Sooner or later, it is likely that you will transform your resistance and take action to go forward, if your long-term commitments and interests will be served by doing so.

Table 4.1 includes gauges of readiness to engage with the steps of valiant leadership. It also contains indications of resistance. The table shows these qualities in juxtaposition because there are times when you may feel ready and also resistant. This may be because you have conflicting priorities; for example, you may not want to "rock the boat" even though you are committed to being an advocate for positive change. You may also feel ready and resistant simultaneously because you do not feel prepared or you are simply not emotionally ready to lead courageously in a given circumstance. The Cycle of Leadership Valor acknowledges these realities: As a leader, you can feel both ready and resistant at the same time. The imperative of Leadership Valor is to be honest, which by definition means that leaders, including you, may not be receptive to change and growth at all times and in every situation.

Here are some important tips to keep in mind as you read through Table 4.1:

- ❖ You may have one or more of the indications of readiness or resistance.

- ❖ You do not need to answer "yes" to all the possible indications in order to claim that you are ready or resistant.

- ❖ There is nothing wrong with identifying with one or more descriptions of resistance.

❖ Remember that progressing through the four steps in order and in depth is not necessary when you are already an expert in a given leadership context. However, you may choose to invoke the steps anyway because doing so will strengthen your effectiveness.

TABLE 4.1 ASSESSING YOUR READINESS FOR THE CYCLE AND THE STEPS OF LEADERSHIP VALOR

	Indications of Readiness	Indications of Resistance
Step 1: *Initiate*	You are willing to stop the action, even for a short pause.	You know you should not do what you are about to do as a leader or manager, but you are going to do it anyway.
	You are comfortable with reflection, thoughtfulness, and perhaps feelings of occasional discomfort as you develop and practice Leadership Valor.	
	You are willing to shift your attention away from circumstances "out there" to yourself.	
	You are willing to consider other actions than the ones that you are tempted to take.	

	Indications of Readiness	Indications of Resistance
Step 2: *Illuminate*	You know there is value in touching base with the fuller sense of who you are as a leader and as a human being. You want a fresh and full-bodied feeling of congruence between who you are and what you are doing. You may feel disconnected from who you are and/or what is truly important to you. You simply feel "off," or less powerful and effective than you usually are. You are aware that one or more of the Seductions has you in its grip. You are ready to face some potentially difficult truths about how the Seductions are influencing you and reducing your effectiveness.	You are aware that one or several Seductions are operating for you, but, at least for now, you are not interested in letting them go or shifting your thinking. You don't have a good sense of who are you at your essence, but you are not interested or willing to ask yourself evocative questions or wait for the answers to emerge. You do not know what your aspirations or dreams are, and, as above, you are not ready to reflect on the possibilities.

continues

TABLE 4.1   ASSESSING YOUR READINESS FOR THE CYCLE AND THE STEPS OF LEADERSHIP VALOR *(CONTINUED)*

	Indications of Readiness	Indications of Resistance
Step 3: *Curate*	You are aware that you have a choice in how you lead, and in selecting the skills and attitudes you bring out in each new circumstance. You are willing to stand up for and articulate what you believe is right, even when it is difficult. You know that leadership requires making adjustments from time to time. You accept that discerning if, when, and how to make shifts in your leadership is part of being valiant.	You remain firm in your strategy, even when new information suggests that adjusting your approach will yield better outcomes.
Step 4: *Integrate*	You have many responsibilities, yet you know that taking time to learn and reflect is central to evolving your leadership. You are willing to think about important leadership challenges that you have experienced so you can identify what you did that worked and what you did that was not as effective.	The demands of your professional life are too great for you to afford any time for reflection and learning. Even if you could find the time for this type of reflection, you do not choose to do that at this time.

As you read the indicators of both readiness and resistance in Table 4.1, how did you fare? Take a moment to read through the next Guidepost to find out.

YOU, LEADING VALIANTLY

1. Think about a particularly sticky situation that is on your plate right now.

   ❖ Are you completely ready, largely resistant, or both resistant and ready to lead valiantly?

   ❖ What do your answers tell you about yourself, and do you like what you see? If not, how can your vision of yourself as a valiant leader be of help to you?

2. If you are resistant to leading valiantly—whether in any of the steps or more than one step—it's up to you to decide whether you will go forward anyway. Are you willing to be uncomfortable as you try new approaches to strengthen your leadership?

3. If you would like support, consider who can provide it.

THE WILLINGNESS TO REFLECT

We have seen that a best practice for leading with valor is increasing your awareness of yourself. For most of us, that means taking some time out from engaging in daily life to consider our circumstances.

As noted previously, making a decision to reflect can be difficult and counterintuitive for action-prone leaders. If you are goal-oriented and contemplation is difficult, it can be useful to reimagine what reflection looks like for you. Some leaders like to spend time in nature or listen to music; some like to take long pauses from ordinary life, perhaps retreating to the country or some other private haven. Others like to reflect with family or community members, good friends, or a mentor or coach. Still others keep it simple and opt for short pauses between moments of action during their normal days.

There is no right way to reflect, nor is there a prescribed or better amount of time to spend doing it. Jackie, the leader we met in Chapter 3, went for a walk as she thought about her choices, her essence, and what she most wanted at this stage of her life. Later, at home, she considered all she had learned as she engaged with each of the steps. These are some of the times and places in which Jackie reflected, but you can reflect in whatever ways work best for you.

YOU, LEADING VALIANTLY

1. Think about the following questions:
   - ❖ What does reflection mean for you?
   - ❖ What do you gain when you reflect?
   - ❖ What are your favorite ways to reflect?
   - ❖ Where do you like to think about important questions?
   - ❖ How often do you allow time to nurture yourself in these ways?

2. Are you satisfied with your answers? If your answer is "no," what will you do to create more opportunities to reflect and nurture yourself and your growth as a leader?

THE WILLINGNESS TO FAIL, ON OCCASION

The idea of failing is difficult for successful leaders to accept. Yet tolerating and even encouraging the reality of trial and error, which is a form of calibration, is central to many successful businesses and venture capital firms (Tian & Wang, 2011). Leaders who are honest about approaches that did not work learn more and earn respect from their colleagues. They also emulate business cultures of excellence and model integrity for those who are watching.

THE WILLINGNESS TO NOT KNOW, UNLEARN, AND BE IMPERFECT

Part of the journey of Leadership Valor is learning how to question assumptions, receive feedback, and let go of what is no longer working. While many healthcare leaders embrace these ideas conceptually, it can be difficult to put them into practice, especially with the press of everyday demands. When it comes to letting go of what worked before or admitting that we have made mistakes, we can be reluctant to face the truth.

But if we are willing to grow and to change by admitting errors and lapses in judgment when they occur, we are embracing the inherent humility of the human condition: We are all works in progress. How we incorporate this wisdom into our way of leading can be challenging, as every seasoned leader knows. This struggle persists despite the theories of learning and unlearning that abound in sophisticated leadership circles, and despite the examples innovative companies provide. In fact, many organizational cultures do not tolerate—let alone embrace—admissions of error or shifts in style or substance of leadership. Failure, mistakes, acknowledgment of problems, or indications that leaders are less-than-perfect can create serious ripples and erode confidence. In addition, the business of healthcare is the business of caring for people. Mistakes in providing that care can be costly beyond measure.

"Part of the journey of Leadership Valor is learning how to question assumptions, receive feedback, and let go of what is no longer working."

Yet many wise healthcare leaders skillfully walk the line between "knowing it all" and "not knowing enough." These are the valiant leaders who reap the benefits of owning both the depth of their expertise and the limits of that expertise. They know that leading authentically and with integrity means they don't know it all. Leading from that stance requires confidence, skill, and willingness to risk not having all the answers every time. Leading courageously can be dangerous in organizational settings that don't stand behind risk taking. But, just as often, leading with valor promotes deep respect and trust among peers, colleagues, and staff.

Valiant leaders make the conscious choice to be honest and authentically humble. This choice is distinctly different from habitually, and perhaps unconsciously, admitting less rather than more about results that are not as good as expected.

YOU, LEADING VALIANTLY

1. Think about times in your life when you have been willing to let go of behavior that served you previously but was no longer helpful. How did it feel to do that, and what opportunities did that create for you?

2. Consider whether there have there been times in your life as a leader when you have said "I don't know," or "I don't know, but I will find out."

    ❖ What was that experience like for you?

    ❖ How often do you do that?

    ❖ How do others react?

3. Consider times in your life when you have not been as successful as you or others hoped.

    ❖ What happened?

    ❖ What did you learn from these experiences?

4. How willing are you to try new approaches now?

5. What support would be useful to you?

6. Can you offer yourself the same level of compassion you give your family and friends when they are not perfect?

THE WILLINGNESS TO BE BRAVE

The word *valor* is built on a foundation of bravery and it reflects what many leaders know is required to lead with vision and conviction. Organizational forces and relationship dynamics are powerful, and without a personal "stake in the ground," it can be very difficult to stay true to who you are and what you are trying to achieve. This is true even for you and other healthcare leaders, despite the caring component of your role and our industry.

Bravery in this context does not mean brash behavior, confidence bordering on narcissism, hubris, or the appearance of personal impenetrability. Instead, valiant leadership embraces bravery that is about standing up for one's principles. It is also about demonstrating the willingness to not be certain on occasion. Valiant leadership encompasses being brave enough to not be an expert at all times, and to learn, unlearn, change, grow, experiment, practice, fail at times, and to accept that as human beings, we are not perfect.

BEING VALIANT

"Valiant leadership embraces bravery that is about standing up for one's principles. It is also about demonstrating the willingness to not be certain on occasion."

Bravery is the ability and willingness to exhibit courage and fortitude. As such, bravery can serve as the antidote to feeling victimized, whether by bosses, co-workers, forces that are bigger than we are, our own stories, or all of the above. When valiant leaders are brave, they do not feel like victims and they do not act like victims. Instead, they experience and exude a sense of honor and completeness. This is true even if the experience did not go as planned.

Brave and valiant leaders guide with the full measure of who they are. Leadership Valor requires bravery to admit one is not perfect, to keep learning, to let go of what is not working, and to encircle rather than shun one's humanity and imperfection.

The Masai, the African tribe, embody a culture of bravery. Theirs is a society that takes courage seriously; it is a culture based on discipline, focus, and self-regulation. While Leadership Valor in healthcare is not about emulating an African tribe, we can learn a great deal from their intentional strategies for self-regulation. At the heart of their strategies is the notion of choice rather than impulse, just as Leadership Valor also supports choice over reactivity.

THE WILLINGNESS TO PRACTICE

What does it mean to practice leading with valor? *Practice* is the work you engage in to develop a skill and a way of being that allows you to embody valiant leadership as you define it. Practicing Leadership Valor is not only about "time spent," as Anders Ericsson, Michael Prietula, and Edward Cokley (2007) emphasized in their

Harvard Business Review article titled "The Making of an Expert." Rather, Leadership Valor calls for what Ericsson and colleagues call "deliberate practice." When cultivating valiant leadership, that practice involves:

- ❖ Making mindful choices about what you do as a leader, and how you do it

- ❖ Practicing leading valiantly in small ways daily, and in big ways when the stakes are high and you are ready, or ready enough

- ❖ Choosing to do that which you do not know how to do well when it is the "right thing to do"

- ❖ Experimenting so you can learn from trial and error

BEING VALIANT

"*Practice* is the work you engage in to develop a skill and a way of being that allows you to embody valiant leadership as you define it."

As noted in Chapter 3, Leonardo da Vinci firmly believed in practice and experimenting so he could incorporate the best of several perspectives into his final masterpieces. Another example of a master who experimented until the end of his life is Phillip Johnson, the renowned architect who crafted huge, elegant structures in New York, San Francisco, and elsewhere. His home in New Canaan, Connecticut, is the living embodiment of practice on a grand scale. The structures on his land represent his forays into different architectural forms, even when they were out of favor in the world of design. The results are stunning representations of art and function. None of these would have been possible had Johnson been unwilling to practice with styles that were unfamiliar and even antithetical to the popular views of architecture at the time.

We practice each time we go around the spiral. When we as leaders consciously think about what we learn in each experience of the cycle, we can adjust what we do the next time and reap the benefit of practice.

Some leaders find it tough to try out new approaches and unfamiliar skills on their own. As noted earlier in this chapter, getting better at leading with valor is easier when we have support from trusted colleagues, peers, friends, family members, mentors, or coaches.

WHAT IS THE VALUE OF PRACTICE WHEN LEADING VALIANTLY?

❖ Leadership Valor is not only a way of being; it is also a leadership skill. Like any skill, you will increase your ability by practicing.

❖ Practice is a tangible, concrete activity. Without practice, learning and thinking about Leadership Valor might be interesting, but they will not lead to any change in your leadership effectiveness. Change *may* happen if you think differently; change *will* happen if you do things differently, too.

❖ As you become clearer about who you are and what you want to achieve, you will get better at bringing forward those parts of yourself—in appropriate measure. *Appropriate measure* means that through practice, you will identify the right times

times and places to manifest what is relevant about your essence and aspirations. Sometimes those parts of you will be quite relevant, and at other times, they will be largely irrelevant. For example, your essence and aspirations may not be immediately pertinent when you are conducting a performance review. However, if you are intent on conducting that same review with tactful consideration and focusing on that staff member's long-term growth, your delivery could be greatly influenced by who you are at your core.

❖ The more you practice leading with valor, the more adept you will be at using the cycle. There will be times when simply remembering the steps will be sufficient; a quick reminder will bring you back to the person you want to be in a given interaction. (We will explore this more fully in Chapter 5, "How to Use the Cycle and the Steps of Leadership Valor.")

❖ Practice with calibration will give you confidence as you take in new information and reconsider your positions from time to time. Calibrating in theory can sound like encouragement to be wishy-washy. Calibrating in practice is far from being wishy-washy; this natural way of operating makes for better decisions and relationships. You can improve the quality of your choices because you can allow new information to influence you—when you think it's appropriate. You will improve your relationships because the people you work with know you are listening to them. Practice allows you to become increasingly fluid and strong (vs. wishy-washy) as you communicate your point of view, whether it is the same or different than it was before.

Going Forward

As we conclude Part I of *Leading Valiantly in Healthcare*, we leave our focus on understanding the theory and practice of Leadership Valor and the examples we have witnessed in Caroline, Jesse, and Jackie.

You now have all you need to move ahead. You know what Leadership Valor is, you have developed your vision for yourself as a valiant leader, and you understand the Seductions and how they can derail you. You have learned about the Cycle of Leadership Valor, the steps you can take, and the rest of the ingredients you need for the journey. Now, it's time to see and practice what Leadership Valor looks like in real life. The stories and exercises in the pages that follow in Part II are designed to help you do just that.

KEY TAKE-AWAYS

❖ While the steps of the Cycle of Leadership Valor are designed to be easy to understand and use, seasoned leaders know that consistent courageous leadership requires more.

❖ Leading with valor takes practice and the ability to manage both readiness and resistance.

❖ Resistance is normal, even when our best interests will be served by courageously moving ahead. Valiant leadership calls for the willingness to be reluctant but to proceed anyway.

❖ Leadership Valor takes the willingness to reflect. Making a decision to reflect can be difficult and counterintuitive for action-prone leaders.

❖ Valiant leadership encompasses being brave enough to not be an expert at all times, and to learn, unlearn, change, grow, experiment, practice, fail at times, and to accept that as human beings, we are not perfect.

PART II
LEADING
VALIANTLY IN
REAL LIFE

In Part I, you learned what Leadership Valor is and what it can mean for you. You saw how several healthcare leaders claimed their innate courage and led more effectively and successfully. In Part II, you will become acquainted with more healthcare stewards who are committed to leading valiantly, even when their circumstances appear to be insurmountable. Like the snapshots in Part I, the stories you will find in Part II are fictionalized. However, the narratives are all inspired by real situations and real leaders who stand up for quality healthcare and leadership excellence in their institutions every day.

In "Leading Valiantly in Real Life," you will find a series of "Vignettes." In some, you will witness leaders who exemplify valiant leadership at its most evolved. You will see others who don't have the same level of skill, commitment, and awareness. They, like many of us, are works in progress. You will observe how they gave into a Leadership Seduction or two, or how they hesitated to lead courageously. You will also learn how they came to terms with their vulnerabilities and reclaimed a more valiant state. Each vignette highlights one or two aspects of Leadership Valor, and although they are grouped by topic, all the stories are "holistic" because they contain other aspects of valiant leadership, too.

This part also contains separate pieces called "Perspectives and Tips." These focus on recognizing and managing the Seductions and the steps in the Cycle of Leadership Valor. Part II concludes with Perspectives and Tips on seeing valiant leadership in others, and recognizing, practicing, and sustaining your own version of spirited, valiant leadership.

Specifically tailored practices and reflective questions are included in each piece. As you think about the exercises and questions, focus on those that offer you the most value. You can read the pieces in Part II in any order and at a pace that allows you to pause and reflect as you wish. What's important is that you take what you need to guide and support you in your real life as a valiant leader.

VIGNETTE 1

SEDUCTIONS IN REAL LIFE

Lynn was a senior leader who was becoming increasingly irritated with Justin, one of the key members of her team. Justin, a highly intelligent Ph.D., was uniquely skilled in his field, and he was asking for more money, more responsibility, and a bigger title. He had started this campaign about a year ago, and, to date, Lynn had resisted his requests. Each time he asked, she said "no" in a way she believed was respectful. At the same time, she felt resentful and troubled by his repeated overtures. While Lynn admired Justin's capability and keen intellect, she also believed he was narcissistic and arrogant.

Lynn was acutely aware that Justin could leave her team and if he did, his departure would create a significant hole in the organization's technical capacity. Because his skills were so well-suited to their needs, Lynn was concerned that it might take quite a bit of time to fill his position with someone equally qualified.

As Justin's requests kept coming, Lynn continued to resist, and the more he asked, the more irritated she became. At one point, she realized that she might be missing an important perspective, but she couldn't yet see what it was. This was bothering her because she knew if she just continued to say "no," she would probably drive Justin out of the organization. If this were to happen, she would not feel at all good about her leadership or the outcome. She was clear that there was a problem between the two of them, and she was willing, even eager, to uncover her part of it. She was committed to leading in an exemplary—and valiant—manner, but she knew she had a way to go when it came to managing an employee like Justin.

WHAT DO YOU NOTICE?

We can easily see that Lynn is having difficulty with the Seductions. Which one(s) do you think she is struggling with?

❖ If you said *Storytelling,* you would be correct. Lynn believes that Justin is arrogant and narcissistic, and this judgmental description may not have any direct bearing on the merits of Justin's promotion request. Nonetheless, it is greatly influencing how Lynn deals with him.

❖ If you said *I Am Right,* you would also be correct. Lynn is holding fast to her labels for Justin, and she is overlaying them on his request for a bigger job and a bigger paycheck.

❖ If you said *It's All About You*, you would be correct again, but only to a certain extent. While Lynn is still somewhat focused on Justin's "faults," she has also started to look at her own role in their impasse. Lynn knows this problem is not exclusively Justin's.

Notice that Lynn is committed to leading valiantly. What is she doing that tells you this?

❖ Lynn realizes that her continued refusals will probably set Justin's departure in motion. Notice that she does not beat herself up when she acknowledges this. Instead, she takes responsibility for the fact that there is a problem, and she is willing to do the work to discover her part in it.

❖ Lynn is doing more than simply saying "no" to Justin. She is also observing and listening to herself. As she does, she grows increasingly certain that there is another way to look at this situation, even though she doesn't yet know what it is.

❖ Lynn is anchored in her knowledge of herself and her commitment to doing what is best for the organization. You can see this value guiding her when she says that she would not feel justified in continuing to say "no" if the cost is that Justin leaves.

WHAT WAS NEXT FOR LYNN?

These last three points attest to Lynn's willingness to back away from a strategy that is not working. Each is an indication of Lynn's readiness to lead valiantly rather than by staying stuck in a position. Together they create a solid foundation for her next steps.

The next move for Lynn was to take herself out of the situation. Instead of just responding to the ever-tempting expediency of the mini-loop (see Figure 3.1 in Chapter 3) and continuing to say "no" to Justin's every appeal, she paused and realized that her approach was neither stopping the requests nor solving the problem.

To prepare to respond differently the next time he asked, Lynn took the first step in the Cycle of Leadership Valor: She chose to Initiate *and reflect. She was determined to keep leading her team as well as possible, and as she moved to Step 2:* Illuminate, *she felt she was clear enough on who she was and what she wanted to achieve in this situation.*

*However, it took some time for Lynn to peel back the layers of the Seductions that had enveloped her. It was very difficult for her to see past her internal, repetitive narrative about Justin (*Storytelling*) and her steadfast commitment to her own point of view (*I Am Right*). Her internal story went something like this:*

"Justin is young and self-centered and wants the promotion because he has a big ego. He excels at the technical aspects of his job, but his people skills are not what they should be. He is already in a role with broad responsibility and if it expands, he will have to take over areas that are competently handled by other team members. Furthermore, he does not need a promotion or more money to keep doing his job; he is in the middle of his salary range, and he is being paid quite well."

Eventually, as Lynn worked this through, she started to see her own prejudices and stereotypes. She realized that Justin's age and tone were coloring her view of his request and his attitude. In addition, his style bothered her because it triggered a bias she had about people who acted as if they were "entitled." Rightly or wrongly, she had been hearing Justin through that filter. In addition, she had been negatively judging him because she would have done it differently if she wanted a raise and a promotion. She realized that her previously unexamined beliefs led her straight into the first Seduction: I Am Right. *As a result, she expected Justin to ask for a raise the way she would have done it.*

Although Lynn was willing to admit that she had been captured by these Seductions, she chose not to indulge in embarrassment that could have stalled her. Instead, she moved on. Lynn thought about other perspectives she could have about Justin. For starters, she reasoned, he was from another generation, and he had different professional concerns than she had at his age. She admitted that being paid more and having a different job title were important to Justin for reasons that Lynn simply did not appreciate.

In moving to Step 3: Curate, *Lynn decided what she needed to do next: talk at greater length with Justin so she could hear his side of the story. She knew that listening openly would not necessarily change her mind. But she also knew that doing so might help her understand Justin at a deeper level and strengthen their relationship.*

Reversing course and asking Justin for a dialogue would take courage on Lynn's part. But as she contemplated this turnaround, she actually felt relieved and even invigorated because she had a plan that honored them both. Lynn was ready and willing to listen and to lead with valor, regardless of what Justin might say.

WHAT ABOUT YOU?

Are there situations in which you, too, have been enticed by beliefs and stories that clouded your judgment and impinged on your best leadership? If so, recall a recent example that still resonates for you.

❖ Remember what happened and which Leadership Seductions took hold.

❖ How did it feel to be drawn in by Seductions in that situation?

❖ How do you think your attitude and actions affected the other people involved?

Lynn realized that her story about Justin and her righteous position were so potent that his departure was almost a certainty unless she did something differently. She also knew that her reaction to his repeated requests was not defensible, because it was neither sound nor well-reasoned. Lynn was able to wake up to these important truths by asking herself the same question you can ask yourself when the Seductions are negatively affecting you and your leadership:

> *"What is happening—or not happening—because of what I am thinking and doing?"*

If and when Seductions do affect you, consider another one of Lynn's key awakenings. In falling for *I Am Right,* she became attached to *how* Justin was asking for a promotion. Notice the irony here: One of her stories about Justin was that he was arrogant, yet Lynn discovered that it was *she* who believed there was just one "right way" to ask for a raise—hers!

VIGNETTE 2

WHEN BEING "RIGHT" TRUMPS GOOD INTENTIONS

Rhea was a successful vice president of a busy metropolitan medical center. Over the years, she had built a large network of strong relationships throughout the organization. While she got a lot of work done through formal channels, she accomplished even more because of her warm, engaging style and her many professional connections with friends and colleagues. At the same time, Rhea had developed a well-organized and finely honed way of carrying out the many facets of her position. She was very clear about her vision for her function and how it served patients and the community. This combination of potent relationships, good organization, a position of relative power, and her unwavering commitment to her vision all contributed to Rhea's signature style and success.

One aspect of Rhea's role was that she oversaw several departments and had a reasonably large number of direct reports. Rhea was quite deliberate in the way she managed these professionals: She had regularly scheduled one-on-one meetings with them and was deeply interested in the intricacies of their functions as well as in their results and their management styles.

To help her stay on top of all the details, she asked all of her direct reports to create the kind of elaborate, multilayered lists she herself used to manage her own responsibilities. She gave them several examples and asked them to use the same format so they could work with these lists in their one-on-one meetings.

Most of her staff members did create the lists, either by using her template exactly as she gave it to them or by modifying it somewhat so it would work for them. Those who made a few modest changes were among those whom Rhea trusted to manage their functions well, so she was comfortable with the alterations they made.

However, one of Rhea's direct reports, Nancy, balked at creating these lists. Nancy's concern was that she did not work with lists like these and to generate them seemed like busywork that she simply didn't have the time to do. When Nancy told Rhea that she would have difficulty fulfilling this request, she also volunteered to give Rhea other information that could help her feel better informed about the details of her work.

Unfortunately, Rhea did not take kindly to what she saw as Nancy's unwillingness to give her what she needed, and she did not want what Nancy proposed instead. Rhea had long felt that Nancy was disorganized, and her resistance to using these lists added *more evidence to her belief. While she acknowledged that Nancy was able to get the job done and achieve excellent results, she was still concerned about Nancy's administrative style, because to her it appeared chaotic.*

Rhea had always been committed to her own leadership develop-ment, and over the years she had invested considerable time and effort to enhance her skills. She was the first to say how much she had learned, but she was not thinking about that as she faced this situation. Instead, she focused on Nancy because she felt quite strongly that Nancy needed to be better organized. Rhea was also committed to getting more information about the particulars of Nancy's functions, and she was sure that getting these lists would give her the level of detail she felt she needed.

What Do You Notice?

Rhea offers a great example of a successful leader who has accom-plished a lot for her organization and the community. She also pro-vides an instructive picture of an executive who has benefitted from her commitment to her own development as a leader. For example, her clarity about her vision and its effect on her work is obvious and compelling. We can surmise that Rhea is so clear because she has a good idea of who she is and what she most cares about as a person and as a professional. She knows what she wants to achieve (her aspiration), so Rhea has not only done the work of Step 2: *Illuminate*, but she has also assimilated the value of that work so it can serve as her leadership foundation; you will recognize that act as Step 4: *Integrate*.

Here are some of the striking features of this vignette:

❖ Rhea's signature flair is usually an asset that contributes to her success on the job. But, like any strength, Rhea's robust style can become a liability when overdone. In this case, Rhea is "forcing" her way of doing things on someone else.

❖ Most leaders know that requiring savvy direct reports to do things "their way" is neither necessary nor good management practice. We can imagine that Rhea knows this, too, but she appears to have forgotten it in this situation. Why might that be? As a valiant leader, isn't Rhea committed to fostering the growth of others in ways that work best for them?

❖ Rhea overlooks the importance of supporting Nancy's growth on her terms because Rhea has been thoroughly captured by the first Seduction, *I Am Right*. Rhea's way of being productive is to work with multilayered lists, but that organizational tool does not work for Nancy. Because Rhea has been hijacked by this Seduction, she can't recognize her excessive attachment to her way of doing things and that her methods are simply not productive for Nancy.

❖ Notice too, that Rhea's need to have it her way precludes her from acknowledging what Nancy presents as an alternative. Significantly, Nancy does not resist Rhea's request for more information; in fact, she offers to give her boss what she wants, but in a way that does not take her offtrack. However, Rhea is not able to step back and calibrate (Step 3: *Curate*) her approach to Nancy.

❖ Like many Seductions, Rhea's version of *I Am Right* has layers that are not immediately obvious. There are at least two other levels in Rhea's rendition of this Seduction.

• Rhea doesn't just want Nancy to create lists for her. Rhea wants Nancy to be better organized, and she believes the lists can help Nancy achieve this goal. Notice that the goal is Rhea's, not Nancy's. Notice, too, that Nancy is a proven professional who routinely produces needed results. Unfortunately, Rhea is unable to see these important facts because she is so focused on the *way* Nancy achieves the results, rather than the results themselves.

• Rhea also asks for the lists because she wants to know more about the details in Nancy's area. Perhaps there are good reasons for this, but it is also likely that Rhea is just too focused on minute aspects of Nancy's job that should not concern her. We have no reason to think that the particulars of Nancy's job are tripping her up or causing difficulties for patients or anyone else. While psychological analysis is not our concern, we might surmise that Rhea has control needs that are influencing her conviction that she is right to want so many details.

WHAT WAS NEXT FOR RHEA?

We left Rhea when she was at an impasse with Nancy, and we rejoin her as she considered her next steps.

Rhea had a long-standing practice of examining and enhancing her leadership choices and challenges. Over the years, she had tried many ways of doing this, and the way that worked best for her was to have a bimonthly meeting with her executive coach. So, instead of confronting Nancy right away, Rhea decided to discuss this challenge with her coach.

She had been working on her leadership for so long that within minutes of starting that conversation, Rhea realized that she, like most of us, fell back into old habits more often than she would like. But she knew old ways die hard for everyone, so instead of giving herself a hard time about it, she had quite a laugh. She immediately understood she was stuck in her version of I Am Right. For her, that translated into "I must be me," and "My way of doing this is the only way of doing this."

Very quickly, Rhea recalled her commitment to leading valiantly. She remembered the Cycle of Leadership Valor, and she revisited what she was about and what she most wanted. She also reminded herself about her susceptibility to the Seductions. This time, she was able to appreciate the value of practice because literally within minutes of initiating a dialogue with her coach, Rhea grasped exactly what she was doing. She quickly realized that needing to be "right" was preventing her from leading in a way that would be more effective with Nancy.

Rhea was clear that she did not want to continue to succumb to "being right" at the expense of being wise, so she created a quick intervention to have when she was tempted again. It involved saying some version of these things to herself:

"This approach isn't working but you want to persist anyway. Why?

Be honest!

And, if you could make this strategy work, what would you get out of it?

Be honest!

And, why isn't what you're doing now working?

Be honest about that, too!"

Rhea did a trial run by using these questions to examine how she was approaching Nancy. Her first answer was that what she had done wasn't working with Nancy because Nancy wouldn't cooperate. But she wanted to be even more honest, so she asked herself again. The second time revealed the real issue:

"This isn't working because you are insisting that Nancy work the way you work, and that isn't the way she does things. You might not like how she does it, but Nancy is successful anyway."

Once Rhea had a new plan to address the temptation of being right, she felt much better. But she didn't stop there. She moved into Curate *and devised a new approach to take with Nancy so she could share her concerns and also honor Nancy's considerable success.*

After creating a better strategy for working with Nancy, Rhea was eager to meet with her again, but before she did, she Integrated *by reviewing what she had learned. She acknowledged that her previous investment in her own leadership growth had yielded many benefits: She knew who she was, what was important to her, and that she could quickly recover when the Seductions became so compelling that she lost her way. She had even established a few questions to ask herself when* I Am Right *had her in its grip.*

WHAT ABOUT YOU?

As you leave this vignette, consider the following questions:

❖ Are there elements of Rhea's story that hit home for you? For example, do Seductions get in your way too, even though you know you shouldn't lead or manage in the way you are?

❖ Are you clear on your Three Levels of Reality (consensus, essence, and dreaming), and do you stay aware of and connected with them? If not, what can you do to remind yourself about the whole of who you are, including your vision and purpose for your work?

❖ What other aspects of Rhea's story hold wisdom and guidance for you?

WHEN BEING "RIGHT" IS MORE IMPORTANT THAN BEING FIRED

Maria had been in a senior position in her not-for-profit institution for a long time, and she had grown comfortable in her role. She felt she had mastered the intricacies of running her part of the organization. Nonetheless, she continued to be fully engaged with the work and the challenge of orchestrating long-lasting and significant results.

Over the last 8 years, Maria had four bosses. While she felt capable of managing much of the stress that this amount of change created, she was less sanguine about their varying methods for reviewing her performance. Still, she thought she had done well enough with her bosses' unpredictable approaches until Tom, the most recent

CEO, arrived. Shortly after Tom was hired several years ago, Maria had her first review. Tom was clear that accurate measures of organizational outcomes were extremely important to him. In concert with new institution-wide efforts to obtain better metrics, Tom wanted Maria and her team to improve the accuracy of measuring the outcomes of their services, too. He encouraged Maria to learn about the organization's commitment to this initiative and to study the fine points of the quantification system he was mandating.

Maria felt she understood what Tom wanted, and she went about the painstaking work of learning about and implementing this new system. She engaged a consultant, and together with the other team members, they put the requisite underpinnings in place over the course of the following year. By Maria's next performance review, the infrastructure was installed, some metrics were available, and more were on their way.

Maria was more than surprised when Tom was not satisfied with her to-date progress. In fact, Tom was visibly frustrated and even more abrupt than usual. Unfortunately, Tom had only 30 minutes for their meeting, and in that time, he did not articulate precisely what was missing in Maria's efforts. His lack of specificity left Maria with unclear guidance about what to do differently. Tom did, however, make it patently clear that he expected improvement by the next written evaluation.

Maria left the meeting feeling angry. As she reflected on their time together and Tom's call for progress, she became even angrier. She was upset because Tom had never acknowledged the good work Maria and her staff had done throughout the year. Maria wanted praise for their achievements, but Tom was a tough boss and did not offer commendation easily. Maria was confident that she knew how to do her job and that she had done what Tom asked of her. She also felt she and her staff knew how to customize the organization's measuring system so it would accurately capture the most relevant data for their services, and she questioned whether Tom truly understood what he was requesting.

But Maria persevered. She signed the written performance document, adding only modest comments, and she tried to perfect the measuring system even though she was not clear about how to change it in a way that would satisfy Tom. In the ensuing months, she privately grew more convinced of Tom's lack of knowledge about her areas of responsibility and the intricacies of a system that would best measure their outcomes. By the time her third performance evaluation with Tom was scheduled, Maria was entrenched in her belief that Tom "didn't know what he was talking about," and that her own actions were above reproach.

WHAT DO YOU NOTICE?

Our first question is whether Maria is enmeshed with any of the Leadership Seductions. What do you think?

If you said, "Yes, she's completely taken with *It's All About You,*" you are correct. If you also identify *Storytelling,* you are right again. And if the title of this vignette points you in the direction of *I Am Right,* you are correct again. Maria is entangled in a substantial way with that one, too.

How realistic do you think this story is? Unfortunately, this type of scenario is not uncommon. A lot of us can understand and empathize with Maria's frustration about the poor performance review process in her organization, as well as the number of bosses she has had in recent years. We can also appreciate that she is probably proficient in her work, and she undoubtedly knows a lot about the data requirements involved in sophisticated outcome measurement systems. It is highly likely that she is skilled enough to supervise the implementation of this system in concert with the organization's overall commitment.

Given these probabilities, we might conclude that Maria is "right" to be stuck on "being right." However, the legitimacy of her conviction is also her Achilles' heel. The ironclad certainty of her belief and the stories that accompany it are building, and as they do, they are blinding Maria to the rest of the picture. She, like many leaders, is so taken with her own certainty that she has no desire to learn anything more about Tom's perspective. Unfortunately, Maria is locked into her "rightness" and as a result, she can't acknowledge that just over the horizon is the very real possibility that she will be fired.

The issue isn't that Maria is right; it is that she is inexorably fused with being right. Regardless of Tom's actual knowledge of the subject, Maria is unwilling to give him another chance to provide input. She is not even asking for more information, regardless of how helpful she thinks the conversation might be. We know Maria is angry, but she may also be frightened about the prospect of being terminated. Instead of speaking up, she is taking a route comprised of a potent combination of silence and Seductions.

WHAT WAS NEXT FOR MARIA?

We can probably empathize with the difficulty Maria had in seeing, let alone understanding, the importance of unwinding her steadfast commitment to her own virtuous position. Fortunately, despite the difficulty, she made a different choice.

Maria stepped back and chose to Initiate *and reflect before it was too late.*

It took some work, but eventually Maria realized that the problem was not that she believed in herself and how she was managing the need for better data. The problem was that she had been so stuck in her righteousness that she could not see the importance of any other point of view. Ultimately, Maria realized she could still believe in the quality of her own work and her correct approach to it, while simultaneously being open to Tom's guidance about the improvements he wanted to see.

Her recognition of the Seductions and their consequences helped her move on to Step 3: Curate *so she could change her strategy and craft a better plan. As she created a new approach to this tough situation with Tom, she began to reclaim her bravery and bolster her confidence, too.*

When she sat down with Tom for her next performance review, she presented a clear picture of her accomplishments and asked Tom for specific guidance about how she could improve her results. Maria was genuinely surprised to find out that Tom had many keen insights and legitimate suggestions and that he knew much more than it seemed at the outset. In fact, their discussion was so helpful that Maria asked Tom for regular progress check-in meetings in the months that followed.

These meetings did not turn out to be lengthy, but they were sufficient to provide the "touch base" that gave Maria regular input and feedback from Tom. Of equal importance, Tom saw that Maria was committed to listening to him and delivering the strong metrics the organization required.

WHAT ABOUT YOU?

The key lesson Maria's story offers is that when we are so convinced of our own superior position, we can slip into the belief that our perspective is the one and only truth. We are simply unable to see that no matter how "right" we are, that truth is still only our truth. It is not *the* truth. This can be a very difficult reality to grasp, let alone accept. But in fact, no matter how justified our position is, other people have points of view, too. It is up to us to be open enough to ask ourselves whether we want to, or ought to, hear any other perspective so at the very least, we can evaluate its merit.

As we leave this vignette, consider these final questions:

❖ If you identify with Maria, what does her experience suggest about your leadership?

❖ What else does Maria's story reveal to you about yourself?

❖ Have you ever been so convinced that you were "right" that you were unable to see some important, even obvious, facets of your situation?

- If so, what happened?

- What were the consequences of being taken by Seduction 1: *I Am Right*?

- What did you learn from that situation?

REALIZING YOU MAY BE WRONG ... EVEN WHEN YOU'RE SURE YOU'RE RIGHT

Vignettes 1, 2, and 3 illustrate what the first Seduction, *I Am Right,* looks like in the everyday life of a healthcare leader. One of the difficulties of this Seduction is that there are many times when we as leaders are, in fact, experts, and we have earned the right to "be right." Our concern with this Seduction is not with that kind of in-depth skill and know-how. Instead, our concern is with the righteous indignation that occurs when we not only claim our expertise but we also let it become so prominent that it's all we see. When that happens, we lose our objectivity and possibly our effectiveness because we have lost interest in anyone else's viewpoint.

Indulging in *I Am Right*, perhaps more than the other Seductions, can be like taking an ego-soothing drug. Vignettes 1, 2, and 3 show us that, as leaders, we can become too convinced about how right we are. Ironically, this über-knowledgeable stance can seduce us right into unconsciousness. In fact, as Maria's story in Vignette 3 shows, we can become so oblivious to the effects of this Seduction that we will even risk losing our jobs before we question the wisdom of our stance. The material below can help you avoid the pitfalls of this powerful Seduction.

LEARN FROM THE RECENT PAST

If you have ever been drawn into *I Am Right*, pick a recent example that's emotionally fresh. Recall the experience as vividly as you can and think about these questions:

❖ If your commitment to being right was rooted in your expertise, consider whether you used your strength in a way that served you well in that situation.

❖ What were the costs of your insistence that your wisdom was paramount? Think about the costs in three ways: the business costs, the social/interpersonal costs, and the costs to you personally.

❖ Does this situation remind you of other times when leading with or owning that same strength in full-Seduction force was not to your advantage?

❖ How can you use the answers to these questions to guide you toward more valiant, Seduction-free leadership in the future?

Intervene in the Moment

If you are prone to *I Am Right*, and if you can catch yourself when you are starting to feel righteous, try these approaches to turn the situation around before it sabotages your success.

Acknowledge Yourself

Honor your feelings, your knowledge, and your skill. Give yourself a genuine pat on the back for your accomplishments. Also give yourself a high-five for noticing *I Am Right* before it takes hold.

Think About Your Impact

Ask yourself how those around you are going to perceive you if you are forceful with your point of view. Does your conviction of your rightness offer the best leadership strategy? If not, what would be better?

Redirect Your Focus

Learn to shift your attention by practicing. Put your expertise and your certainty on the back burner, at least for a while. Reframe by asking what's important. Or, direct your awareness away from yourself and toward the situation and others who are involved. See if you can summon interest in their perspectives.

Ask a Question

When all else fails, stop yourself from making any statement at all. Instead, ask a question, and when you can, make it a genuinely curious one. Maria's revised approach to Tom in Vignette 2 illustrates the power of a question. When she sat down with him for her third performance review, she presented him with her accomplishments. Then, she specifically asked him for guidance that would help improve her results. That question, and her openness to his answer, changed the course of the conversation and their relationship from that point on.

Remember Your Essence and Aspirations

Lean into your Three Levels of Reality rather than just your go-to belief about what's happening in the moment, right in front of you (consensus reality). Notice what happens when you refocus and include more perspectives than just what's immediate, and consider the following questions:

- ❖ What do you remember when you do this?

- ❖ Is being right still of primary importance?

- ❖ If something has shifted, what has become more important?

- ❖ How does the answer about what's important affect your impulse to lead with the view that you are inexorably right?

- ❖ Are you going to do anything differently? If so, what?

VIGNETTE 4

THE DESTRUCTIVE POWER OF *STORYTELLING*

Lupe was settling into a new job that she was initially very excited to have. When she took the position, she was sure her new role would give her an opportunity to make a substantial contribution to her field. The organization represented a new healthcare setting for Lupe, and she had never worked in an environment quite like it before. However, as she grew familiar with the job, its requirements, and her new colleagues, she found that adjusting to so many changes was far more taxing than she had anticipated.

From the start, Lupe worked very hard, putting in frequent late nights and weekends at the office. She said she did this because she believed she could truly excel in this job by doing whatever it took, including working many hours. Unfortunately, during her first 6 months in the position, Lupe also ate too much, stopped exercising, and grew by two dress sizes. She also didn't spend much time with her family.

Despite her dedication and hard work, as Lupe went into her seventh and eighth months on the job, she felt less rather than more successful. Her mood darkened, and she became pessimistic about her ability to keep up with the many expectations of her position. She grew listless and withdrawn, even as she endeavored to do it all "perfectly" by continuing to keep long hours and work most weekends.

Privately, Lupe lamented how she was faring compared to the success she had enjoyed in her previous leadership roles. She had always been a hard worker and had been widely acknowledged for her achievements. Needless to say, Lupe was more than a little troubled by her current difficulties. It didn't help that her boss saw many of the same problems that Lupe did; her assessment of her own performance was not distorted.

Lupe had still another concern: She was feeling that her boss was not a good leader, and she was gathering many examples to prove her point.

WHAT DO YOU NOTICE?

Lupe started her new job with a clear idea of who she is and what she wants to accomplish, so it appears that she has a good grasp of the first part of Step 2: *Illuminate*. But is she, in fact, opting for valiant leadership?

❖ As much as Lupe might want to be a valiant leader, she is not headed in that direction. Notice that as time passes, Lupe is faced with more work and greater challenges. Despite months of effort that are not producing the results she wants, Lupe does not elect to *Initiate* and reflect on what she is doing. Instead, Lupe responds by doing the same thing repeatedly: She works harder and longer, even as she grows more tired and discouraged.

❖ While seeking perfection is not specifically named as one of the Six Leadership Seductions, it can be a root cause for several of them. Lupe's way of striving for perfection reveals just how compelling—and counterproductive—reaching for this unattainable goal can be. The quest to be "perfect" is quite common, especially among ambitious leaders.

❖ Lupe is caught in the mini-loop of expediency. Her rationale is that she can not only succeed but also excel in her new job if she just works hard enough. But success is not forthcoming; instead, Lupe finds herself in a repeating cycle of working too much while growing further behind, more fatigued, and less successful.

❖ Lupe is stuck in the second Seduction: *Storytelling*. She is telling several stories that are literally taking over her ability to think clearly and see the self-destructive cycle she is in. Her stories start with a focus on herself, and they come in two forms: Some are words she says to herself, and others are beliefs that motivate her behavior. These beliefs and narratives build on each other and create the reality she is experiencing. They go something like this:

> *"If I just work hard enough, I will not only succeed but I will also excel."*

"I have always been successful before, so I should be successful now even though this environment and these circumstances are completely new to me."

"What was true in the past should be true now."

"It's okay to not take care of myself."

❖ Notice that because Lupe does not challenge or interrupt any of these stories, they increase in potency and spawn more Seductions. Over time, these additional Seductions take hold, too:

 • Lupe *Checks Out*. Despite putting in lots of time in the office, she becomes listless and withdrawn, and we can be certain that she is not optimally productive during at least some of the hours she spends at work.

 • Lupe is also taken with the last Seduction, *It's All About You*. She doesn't feel her boss is supportive of her many efforts for their organization. While we don't know that she blames him for her lack of success, we do know that she is saying things about him in her own mind that are, at the very least, undermining the productive potential of their relationship.

WHAT WAS NEXT FOR LUPE?

Once Lupe decided to do the work of an aspiring and valiant leader, here's what she did.

First, Lupe shut down her fruitless—and endless—recycling of the mini-loop of expediency. Instead, she chose the Cycle of Leadership Valor. Lupe knew she would benefit from greater self-awareness when she took the first step, Initiate. *Just doing this allowed her to feel a little calmer because, even if for a moment, she stilled her constant need to work hard. Instead, she paused.*

Next, she invoked the first part of Illuminate *and looked at what was truly important to her, not just professionally, but personally, too. She reconfirmed what had been true throughout her life: As eager as she was to contribute to her profession, she was at least as eager to maintain her health and to spend time with her family.*

Lupe realized that she was engulfed in stories about herself that were destructive to her success and well-being. As soon as she realized that she was giving these stories too much power, she decided she wanted to create new ways of thinking that were more supportive of her and her good health. For example, one of Lupe's new narratives emphasized listening to her body and reminding herself that she was on the right track when she paid attention to her feelings.

In moving on to Step 3: Curate, *Lupe identified facets of her skillset that could help her be more successful in her new role, and she developed a plan to use them. One of her proven strengths as a leader was her ability to tackle problems head on; that's what she originally wanted to do with this position and with her boss, too. So, a key aspect of Lupe's updated plan involved having a serious discussion with him, and that's just what she did.*

146

Lupe felt great about initiating that dialogue. It was productive, and it cleared the air between her and her boss. But in the weeks immediately following their meeting, Lupe did not feel any more successful with her projects, and she began to feel that her relationship with her boss was deteriorating all over again.

This time, Lupe knew she needed to regroup much more quickly than she had before. Because she had Integrated *her learning from her earlier work with the cycle, she knew how to avoid falling into the ill-serving but compelling pull of the mini-loop.*

Instead, she decided to start with Initiate *again. She thought carefully about what to do. She reminded herself what she most wanted to accomplish at this point in her life. She was proud that she had not immediately fallen into dysfunctional* Seductions, *and she moved onto* Curate. *She looked especially at calibration, and as she did, she asked herself,*

> "Should I shift my approach, and if so, in what way?"

> "Or should I go back to working just as hard as I did when I first started the job?"

> "Or should I choose another direction altogether?"

Eventually, Lupe took the last option and chose something completely different. She decided to leave the job. She reasoned that her health and family relationships would continue to suffer, and she no longer believed that this job was a good fit. Although she was saddened that her original dream would not be realized, she felt much more aligned with herself, her family, what was important

147

to her, and her new dream going forward: to be in good health and to be close with those she loved most.

WHAT ABOUT YOU?

Lupe's story reveals the power of asking these questions when you are feeling stuck:

❖ Is there a story (or more than one) that is leading you, instead of the other way around? If so, what is it?

❖ If you are caught in the mini-loop of expediency, what are the compelling narratives or beliefs that are driving you?

❖ How are your stories helping or not helping you go where you want to go in your leadership life?

You can also use Lupe's journey as a catalyst to reflect more generally about the stories you tell yourself:

❖ What narratives influence you and your leadership the most?

❖ In what ways do these stories serve you, and in what ways do they not serve you?

❖ In what ways can you adjust your stories so they are more accurate, more empowering, and more apt to sustain you as a valiant leader?

As we leave this vignette, we can take its biggest lesson with us: As valiant leaders, it is our work to create stories that are accurate and that empower rather than diminish us.

SIX STORIES THAT KEEP US STUCK

"The truth you believe and cling to makes you unavailable to hear anything new."
—Pema Chödrön

As described in Chapter 2, *Storytelling* is a Leadership Seduction when our stories grossly exaggerate or minimize the facts, when they are exceedingly difficult to relinquish, and when they preclude us from honoring any perspective other than our own. "Honoring" another perspective does not mean we like or agree with it. It simply means that we are open to hearing it. Even when they do not reach the Seduction threshold, our stories can still limit our openness because they can be potent—and blinding—representations of what we believe to be "the truth," as Lupe learned in Vignette 4. Our stories are literally the sum and substance of what we believe is happening in our lives, and as such they influence us and those we lead a great deal.

Because our stories are so important, they deserve special emphasis and understanding within the context of leading valiantly. This vignette describes six narratives that are common among leaders who are doing the work of guiding healthcare every day. Each story also contains a *back story*, which is the rest of the story that can influence us so greatly. The back story may not be said aloud, but it can represent what we think and feel as we tell these stories to ourselves and others.

When you read these stories, think about whether they are similar to your own. Because the details will differ for you, concentrate on the underlying message. See if you relate to that message and if so, consider how it affects you and your capacity to lead valiantly.

Notice, too, whether any of these stories operate as Seductions for you. Remember that these (and all stories) don't become Seductions until they are so "loud" that they block us from hearing anything else. Stories that do not reach the threshold of a Seduction are just narratives we tell ourselves. Whether they are true or not, most of them simply come and go.

As discriminating leaders, we want to be conscious of our stories, both those we tell others and those we tell ourselves. Just because we have a thought does not mean that it is important or valid. The same is true for stories: They are not all of equal value. We don't have to hold onto and retell every story.

Friedrich Nietzsche and other philosophers give credence to this notion by suggesting that there is no such thing as "truth"—there is only point of view (Carlisle, 2003). Just because you have a point of view, it does not have to be permanent, you do not have to be right, and you do not have to stick with it no matter what. You can be discerning about the stories you tell yourself and others. You can also "rewrite" or change them to make them more accurate and supportive of who you want to be as a valiant leader.

If you are a leader who repeats one or more of these tales on occasion, there is nothing to be ashamed of. Valiant leaders are human beings. We have the opportunity to rewrite our narratives so they better match the leaders we are becoming rather than the leaders we have been.

A NOTE OF CAUTION

None of these storylines is pretty. As leaders on our way to becoming valiant, we may not like these statements, and we may not want to admit that we ever tell these or similar tales. But they are included here because some leaders do communicate these stories—either in words, in attitude, in action, or in all three.

STORY #1: PEOPLE DON'T SEE ME

Here are a few of the many variations on the theme of telling yourself you are invisible:

People don't understand me, my competence, my role, my excellence, what I have done, what I am supposed to do, etc.

People don't like me or support me.

BACK STORY

The back story is usually something like:

- ❖ "What is the matter with these people?"

- ❖ "Why don't they recognize how good I am, how hard I've worked, what I've done to train, or how I've helped them?"

WHAT TO NOTICE

This story may be a Seduction if it's long lasting and difficult to release. It's also possible that this is not the primary Seduction; the bigger Seduction could be *I Am Right*. Either way, this is a disempowering story that can lead to all the other Seductions, specifically *Checking Out, It's All About You* (particularly the part about blaming others), *No!*, and *Being Distracted*.

HOW TO REWRITE THIS STORY

A valiant leader can "re-write" this story by changing the internal dialogue to something like this:

> "They're not acknowledging who I am, what I need, or what I can do. No matter what their reasoning is, I am going to manage myself and my emotions. If they misunderstand my role or relevant expertise, I may simply let it go. Or, if I need to take action, I will explain it assertively—versus aggressively. I may also ask for their perspective."

STORY #2: POOR ME

This story comes in many forms. Here are a few of them:

This situation is awful, and there is nothing I can do about it.

I don't have any power here. I am a victim.

Other people have made decisions that I must implement, even though I don't like or agree with them.

BACK STORY

The back story here is usually something like:

* ❖ "I have many reasons and justifications that support the 'fact' that I didn't have anything to do with the circumstances which now victimize me."

* ❖ "This wouldn't have happened if such and such hadn't occurred."

WHAT TO NOTICE

Like Story #1, this narrative will be a Seduction if it is long-lasting and unrelenting. Although an internal dialogue like this can just be a story, it usually isn't. Most often this story is reflective of at least one of the Seductions. It's usually about *I Am Right, It's All About You* (particularly the view that "they did it"), or *Checking Out* ("I have good reasons for checking out.").

How to Rewrite This Story

We can rewrite this story by first being willing to recognize it as part of Step 2: *Illuminate* and then letting it go. We can also examine what our role might be in the situation that is so troubling. If we do have any responsibility for what is happening, as valiant leaders, we will eventually take ownership for the role we have played.

If we do not have anything to do with the situation, we can make the choice of self-awareness (*Initiate*) and discover what is troubling us so much (*Illuminate*). We may have understandable feelings of anger, sadness, or upset if something truly disturbing has occurred. We can honor those feelings, and eventually, when we are ready, we will either act on them, let them go, move on, or all of the above.

As we move on, we will ask ourselves what we can do in this situation: What is in our control? We can take action based on our answers, and as we do, we empower and lift ourselves out of the "poor me" victim stance.

Story #3: It's Your Fault

This story, too, has many versions. Some of them are:

> *Things would be a lot better if you/she/he were different.*

> *There are a lot of problems here, and he/she caused them.*

BACK STORY

The back story is usually something like:

- ❖ "I am fine. It's that person who really needs to change."
- ❖ "Here's what's wrong with that person, and here's exactly what that person needs to do get back on track. If only I or someone could say these things to that person and he/she would cooperate, things would be so much better."

WHAT TO NOTICE

While it is true that this story could just be a simple story, it usually isn't. Most often, this story is both intense and frequent. It usually represents at least one full-fledged Seduction or a combination of them, including *It's All About You* and *Storytelling*. There is often a generous helping of *I Am Right* mixed in as well.

HOW TO REWRITE THIS STORY

As valiant leaders, we take full responsibility for ourselves whenever we can, and in doing so, we realize that there is very little we can do to change or "fix" another person. The best we can do is practice leading in ways that demonstrate our valor, our humanity, and our understanding that we are not perfect and no one else is, either.

Story #4: Drama Trumps Fact

We all know individuals who veer toward the dramatic when they speak. The question is whether this applies to us, too. Here is an example of the way this flair for theater can sound:

> *This happened, and then this happened, and this other thing happened, and she did this and he did that, and in the end, the story I am telling has nothing to do with what actually took place!*

Back Story

The back story goes something like:

❖ "Then this happened, then that happened, and I can't believe it, but these other things happened, too! Can you believe this? And each time I tell this story to someone else or to myself, it gets better and better!!"

❖ "Whether I am conscious of it or not, I love being the center of attention."

What to Notice

"Drama Trumps Fact" exemplifies what can occur when people tell stories. It's all about creating drama, whether a situation deserves it or not. When leaders tell these kinds of stories, they take on a life of their own. Perhaps unconsciously, the leaders stop describing what is real and start engaging in a form of entertainment that puts them in the middle of the action.

HOW TO REWRITE THIS STORY

As leaders, we want to be conscious of the stories we tell and the impact we have when we are telling them. If we are tempted to amplify the gravity of a story so it reaches dramatic levels, we can ask ourselves if this story deserves that treatment. If it doesn't, we can remind ourselves to slow down and share a version of the truth that is closer to what actually transpired. We can do this when we respect ourselves as grounded leaders rather than getting lost in the excesses of entertaining others. From that anchored perspective, we can decide if we want to choose a different way to tell our stories so they are more accurate and less theatrical.

STORY #5: THIS WILL NEVER WORK

Once again, there are many variations on the theme of naysaying. Just a few of them are:

> *I can't. I can't do it.*
> *I'll do what they ask, but it still won't work.*

BACK STORY

The words above often mask a back story that represents one of three levels of resistance as described by Rick Maurer (2009):

❖ The first level is "I don't *get it.*"

❖ The second level is "I don't *like it.*"

❖ The third level, also the most challenging, is "I don't *like you.*"

WHAT TO NOTICE

The sentiments in this story are decidedly negative. Valiant leaders will be aware as they hear themselves say these or similar words to themselves and others. They will also monitor whether they articulate a version of this story frequently and with a great deal of intensity. If so, they are probably manifesting the full-fledged *No!* Seduction.

HOW TO REWRITE THIS STORY

When we are tempted to slip into this story, whether it is a Seduction or not, we can make another choice. Instead of just reacting to a situation that "makes" us feel this way, we can opt to *Initiate*. We do not have to respond like leaders who repeatedly object or feel sorry for themselves. In choosing the Cycle of Leadership Valor, we choose to stop the action, at least momentarily, so we can ask ourselves whether this story and these emotions are taking us where we want to go.

Most importantly, we can ask ourselves whether the story is true, or even somewhat true. Our answers will guide us. Even if we believe we really cannot win and it really will not work, we can lead valiantly. We can lean into our courage, understand who we are at our core, and create a plan for moving forward anyway. We don't have to remain in a sour frame of mind and simply "take it."

STORY #6: IT WAS BETTER BEFORE

Although the specifics vary, the general theme of "It was better before" is always the same. It sounds like this:

> *I long for the good old days.*
>
> *I/we did it that way, the outcomes were great, and that's the way it should be done now.*
>
> *When So and So was here, everything was fine.*
>
> *We didn't have these problems where I worked before.*

BACK STORY

The back story here is something like:

❖ "The way things used to be is much better than the way things are now. I/we/they had it all together, people did what I/we/they wanted them to do, and everything was just fine.

❖ Ever since X happened, things have gone downhill fast."

WHAT TO NOTICE

This story often operates at the level of a Seduction and most often includes both the story itself (*Storytelling*) as well as the conviction that the storyteller is right (*I Am Right*).

HOW TO REWRITE THIS STORY

As valiant leaders, we take seriously the work of staying current and connected with ourselves as we are now. It takes both vigilance and willingness to pay attention to the facts of our current circumstances, as well as the stories we tell about them.

SUSTAINING VALOR IN THE FACE OF *STORYTELLING*

Lupe's story in Vignette 4 and the Perspectives and Tips on the Six Stories That Keep Us Stuck illustrate the power of the narratives we spin in our heads and through our words. So far, we have concentrated on the sway our stories can have on us as leaders. Remember, too, that our stories influence those around us. Chapter 2 captured many of these consequences, including the facts that we can mislead others who depend on us for accurate information and guidance, and that we can lose the respect of our co-workers if our tales are too tall to be believed. Often our colleagues can see truths we cannot see when we are overly enthralled with our own stories. These are serious ramifications, and when coupled with the damage we can do to ourselves as leaders, we can see that *Storytelling* deserves our vigilance. Here are a few tips that can help you keep your stories in check.

ASK, THEN ASK AGAIN

Byron Katie (2002) offers a single question that can ground you in the fullest and most accurate version of reality when you speak:

"Is it true?"

She suggests we ask ourselves that question, and then she suggests we ask it again:

"Is it *really* true?"

ANCHOR YOURSELF IN THE PRESENT

A variation on Katie's question is also important:

"Is it *still* true?"

We have seen how a lack of attention to what is true *now* versus what was true *before* can create problems for us and for others. Staying present to and articulating what is true now versus what was true before anchors you in *current* fact. This allows your valor to shine instead of being hidden by obsolete statements that distort, distract, disempower, and send inaccurate messages.

IDENTIFY FILTERS

If you find yourself moving in the direction of distorted stories, ask yourself whether unhelpful filters might be influencing you. If they are, see if you can identify them. Remember that filters serve as lenses through which we experience events in our lives. They are byproducts of age and generation, upbringing, ethnicity, religious or cultural heritage, and the like. Sometimes filter-based distortion occurs because we inadvertently like or dislike someone or something not because of the facts, but because our filters have turned into biases that reduce our ability to be open minded.

We all have filters and biases, and we can all be affected by them. It is up to you as a valiant leader to consciously decide whether and how you want your biases to influence you and the stories you tell.

CATCH YOURSELF IN THE ACT

If you think you are prone to *Storytelling*, but you're not sure, try this exercise:

1. Think about a big challenge you have right now. (If you don't have one, think about a recent encounter that still has some emotional charge for you.)

2. Think about the details of this challenge. If there is someone you trust and want to engage as you do this exercise, tell him or her what is happening. Give as much detail as you can. If you're alone, just describe the situation to yourself, in writing or aloud in private.

3. As you do this, notice what you are saying. Are you distorting the facts? If you are, take a moment to adjust your narrative so it more closely resembles the truth.

4. Think about what you learned by doing this exercise and take that forward into the next opportunity you have to relay a story.

IDENTIFY YOUR STORY'S PURPOSE

When you tell a story, ask yourself about your purpose for telling it and the goal you want it to achieve.

If you are often tempted by *Storytelling*, you may have more than one right answer to these questions. For example, you might say,

> "I am telling the story because the people I am talking with need to have the information."

While that may be true enough, ask yourself again:

> "Why am I telling this story?"

The second time you may get a different and an equally true answer. For example, you may end up answering something like:

> "I am telling this story because I want these people to think that I am a smart, powerful, and influential leader."

Pay Attention to Your Words

When you are telling stories, use language consciously. If you need grounding, tap into your knowledge of yourself and use words and tones that reflect your essence and what you most want as a leader. Let them influence how you describe consensus reality as you see it.

Remember that your words have power not just because of their content, but also because of the emotion you exude and the emotion you evoke. If you're not sure about the impact you have when you tell your version of the facts, ask trusted others for feedback so you can make sure you are conveying the message you want to send.

VIGNETTE 5
DISTRACTION
TWO WAYS

The number of ways we can be sidetracked is probably close to the number of leaders in healthcare and all other fields combined. This vignette includes just two examples of distraction when it has become a full-fledged Seduction. As you read, you will notice similarities and differences in these two leaders—Dee and Sara—and how they allow themselves to fall into *Being Distracted*.

DEE

Although she had a responsible managerial position in a medical center, Dee worked for Henry, a physician leader who was known for his many accomplishments and who, she claimed, was far more powerful than she was. Dee said that most people in the organization saw Henry as "larger than life." Almost everyone admired Henry. Some feared him, too, at least a little.

Dee knew she contributed to Henry's substantial reputation for getting things done. When asked if she, too, was respected by the organization's key leaders, she said yes. However, she believed that her impact was a result of Henry's influence rather than something she had achieved on her own. Dee said she had "positional power": power that was hers only because she worked for Henry.

From time to time, Dee was conscious of diminishing her standing as well as some of her opinions. She said she did this when she believed it was her responsibility to defer to Henry or his view on what was best for the organization. When asked if she wanted to step away from Henry's shadow and take on a bigger leadership role, she said she knew she could handle a larger role, but she wasn't sure she wanted one or was ready for it.

SARA

Sara was a chief executive officer (CEO) who hired Candice, a new senior leader, to join her team a few months previously. Their organization had a great deal of visibility in the healthcare community, and every member of the senior team was under a lot of pressure to perform well. Sara became the CEO 18 months ago when she was promoted from Candice's position. Although Sara was not in trouble in her role as CEO, she found it quite challenging.

Even though Candice was a quick study and showed no sign of being overly taxed by her new job, Sara went into Candice's office 5 or 6 times a week to volunteer advice and guidance. She wanted to hear Candice's plans and review her documents, even when the issues they focused on were not politically sensitive. Sara frequently gave Candice pointers about strategies and tactics that worked for her when she had the job. Sara did not think she was micromanaging; she believed she was mentoring Candice.

WHAT DO YOU NOTICE?

Although their circumstances are different, both Dee and Sara are engaged in some form of "playing small." For their own reasons, they are limiting their potential for valiant leadership by allowing themselves to be taken in by the fourth Seduction, *Being Distracted.* If you noticed that they may also be *Checking Out,* you would also be correct. Although Dee and Sara are both fully engaged with their roles, they have checked out from going the extra mile and offering the full measure of their potential as leaders.

To see how *Being Distracted* is playing out, we need to examine Dee's and Sara's stories more closely.

DEE'S DISTRACTION

❖ Dee is aware that she is supporting another leader's greatness, and she is certain that her own impact is largely, or entirely, referential. In other words, she believes that her influence comes only from her association with her more powerful boss, Henry. She knows that she, too, is making a contribution, but she is settling for a view of herself that lives largely in the shadow of another leader.

❖ When asked if she is ready or willing to move out of that shadow and into a leadership role that is more independent, she hesitates. We don't know all the reasons why Dee doesn't want a bigger role, but we can surmise at least one reason for her reluctance. It is probable that Dee has grown comfortable with letting someone else take the helm. This choice means that she doesn't have to initiate the work and face the challenges that leading valiantly can require.

SARA'S DISTRACTION

❖ Candice does not need or ask for Sara's help, but Sara persists in offering it anyway. Candice has her job under control. Her strategies and communications are effective, and she is not dealing with politically sensitive issues that Sara would rightly want to manage in a hands-on way.

❖ So why is Sara checking in on Candice so much? It's likely that Sara is simply taking it easy when she goes into Candice's office to offer her help. She is telling herself that she is "mentoring" Candice. Sara does not see that she is allowing herself to be distracted by easier tasks that are no longer hers to do. When she "mentors" Candice, she is absolving herself of the more difficult work that awaits her in her own office. For Sara, it's a lot less challenging to do the work of her old job than to step fully into the shoes of being the CEO.

WHAT ABOUT YOU?

Many of us can relate to Dee and Sara because we enjoy the less-taxing aspects of our jobs from time to time. Taking advantage of these moments is normal and human. What turns them into Seductions is focusing on these periods excessively. When we become conscious of the times we are tempted to take the easy way out, we can choose to limit the time we spend playing small or being distracted in other ways.

If you find the lure of *Being Distracted* compelling on more occasions than you would like, ask yourself these questions:

❖ What aspects of Dee's or Sara's story help you see yourself in a different light?

❖ Are there occasions in which you are distracted and your way of leading is less effective than what you are capable of?

  • If so, what are they?

  • What are you doing in those parts of your job, and what stories are you telling yourself about what you are doing?

  • Why are you allowing yourself to be distracted?

❖ Whether you relate to playing small or not, consider the situations in your leadership life in which you are unfocused.

  • What is happening during those times, and what do you do when you are distracted?

- Remember your vision of yourself as a valiant leader.

- Notice the difference between your vision and the times you are allowing yourself to be distracted. Refocus your vision of yourself as a valiant leader on how you want to lead the next time you are tempted by, and don't want to succumb to, *Being Distracted.*

❖ When you are distraction-prone, do you experience congruence between what you are doing in your leadership role and your ambitions and your core as a human being?

- If you don't feel accord within your Three Levels of Reality, where do you feel out of alignment?

- How can the steps and Leadership Valor as a whole bring you back into harmony so you will be less susceptible to distractions?

❖ Notice how often you nurture yourself by taking time away from the hard work that leadership requires. If you find that you don't take many opportunities to renew yourself, you may be setting yourself up to be excessively distracted on the job.

VIGNETTE 6

THE ECHO
CHAMBER
OF TEAM
SEDUCTIONS

The team of nurse managers and directors at a large community hospital was made of up of 20 talented, accomplished, and committed professionals. Together, they had achieved a great deal for their institution, and their Chief Nursing Executive (CNE) was immensely proud of their many successes.

But things started to change when the hospital's leadership embarked on a complex joint venture that called for building a new facility. The new hospital would take 5 years to complete, and as preparations got underway, these managers didn't just become busier, they became "overwhelmingly consumed" with work. They felt they had to keep up with every aspect of their normal workloads while simultaneously developing new partnerships and plans at all levels of service. On top of that, many of them were partici-

pating in designing the new building, too. While they were used to working at full capacity, many were now spending weekends and evenings at the hospital not just occasionally, but all the time.

As a long-standing practice, their CNE brought the team together for bimonthly "retreats." On one such occasion early in the rollout of the new initiatives, nearly everyone in the group complained at length about the many changes that were occurring in their organization. They were very unhappy about their numerous responsibilities in planning for the merged services and the new hospital, too. Their CNE listened for a short time, but soon, she grew visibly impatient. She told them she wanted them to focus on the future and think strategically about the opportunities that these changes offered them, their patients, and their community. On a practical level, she strongly encouraged them to be more proactive and prioritize their responsibilities. She asked them to delegate more, and she urged them to stop working so much in the evenings and on the weekends.

When she told them to delegate, shorten their work hours, and focus on the most important items on their to-do lists, the team members grew even more distressed. Their responses ranged from outright anger to statements like "We can't stop working so much," and "Don't ask us to identify what is most important, because the organization says it's all important."

Historically, the team members had admired their CNE, but at this point they were palpably upset with her. In private conversations, several of them reported that they resented her suggestions about making their lives more manageable because they felt she was sending mixed messages. On the one hand, they were working so hard because "the organization" (read, the CNE) demanded it, and on the other hand, the CNE was saying they should cut back.

WHAT DO YOU NOTICE?

Many of us are all too familiar with this kind of situation. Just hearing about it reminds us of the frustration and genuine difficulty of having too many demands, all of them important, and too little time to attend to every task. This common story offers many insights into the challenges—and possibilities—of leading valiantly.

FORCES AT WORK IN THIS VIGNETTE

Notice how legitimate the stresses of this situation are. The team's responsibilities are so consuming that it appears that these managers have no choice but to work long hours and do whatever it takes, for as long as it takes, to accomplish everything that needs to be done.

Because the demands are real and the stresses are genuine, it is easy to conclude that these managers are truly powerless. It seems that they cannot do anything but give in to the enormous workload, loss of personal time, and the need to be everywhere, doing everything. Notice, too, that this seems to be true even though their boss is telling them to take control of themselves and the situation.

But if you look closely, you can see the "setup" in this vignette. It is that the very compelling demands in the situation seem to call for, and perhaps even "require," the managers to acquiesce. It appears that they must do whatever it takes to get the job done. In other words, they simply must hop into the never-ending mini-loop of expediency and stay in it until the job gets done.

But even in this circumstance, valiant and discerning leaders can step away from the mini-loop and the power of the group, at least for a moment. They will choose to pause, even if it's just in their own minds. When they do this, they will remember that they as individuals—and the team as a whole—are not powerless in this or any leadership situation. Instead of just reacting over and over again, these leaders can *Initiate,* and so can the team. In taking Step 1, they are opting for self-awareness and deeper grounding that can guide their future choices in these stressful circumstances.

Sometimes, a team's strength can become a liability. In this vignette, the team members respect and listen to one another. Unfortunately, in this case, that collective asset leads to a shared belief that they in fact have to work long, long hours and that they are powerless to change, even when the CNE asks them to. The team's close connection has become a liability because they are sharing their emotional reactions to their stressful conditions and as they do, they intensify their feelings.

Notice, too, that the burdens on these managers are not just short-term requirements. Solidifying the joint venture and building the new hospital are 5-year projects. Doing whatever it takes for as long as it takes might be appropriate if this workload were temporary. But these circumstances are anything but transient. It really is imperative that these managers reclaim their power—and their valor—individually and as a group so they can sustain themselves for the long haul.

THE POWER OF COMBINED SEDUCTIONS

As described and illustrated in Chapter 2, Seductions often appear in clusters. Notice that this is true for the team in this vignette.

❖ How many Seductions do you see, and which ones are they?

❖ Is there one Seduction that is primary?

SIX LEADERSHIP SEDUCTIONS

If you suspect that all six Seductions are operating for the individuals on this team, you are exactly right. You would also be right if you suspect that some team members are likely to be enthralled by some Seductions while other team members are entirely absorbed in others. For example, some on the team may be completely taken (and angered) by the story that they "have to work this hard" (*Storytelling*) while others may be so resigned that they feel they have no choice but to give in (and *Check Out*).

This team gives us a clear example of the ways in which Seductions can build on one another. Not only do Seductions frequently appear in clusters, but they can grow stronger when groups of people are involved. When that happens, the Seductions can take over a team's reality unless its members are vigilant.

Here is a brief exploration of ways in which the powerful combination of all the Seductions is operating for this team:

❖ **Seduction 1: *I Am Right*.** We can surmise that most members are convinced they are right and that they have no choice but to work so hard. They firmly believe the facts are on their side, despite their boss's direct request to think differently and change their behavior. The team members feel they are justified in being attached to the belief that they have too much to do and little choice but to do it.

❖ **Seduction 2: *Storytelling*.** Some (or many) team members probably have some version of a story that convinces them that they "have to work this hard," that "this is the way it is," and that "they are powerless" to do anything about it.

❖ **Seduction 3: *Checking Out*.** While they are working so hard, many team members have relinquished their sense of perspective and their belief in their own ability to change the situation. "This is the way it is" is not only a story (as noted in the entry for Seduction 2, above), it is also a conviction that can easily lead to *Checking Out*.

❖ **Seduction 4:** *Being Distracted.* These team members are so distracted by so many compelling circumstances (a new hospital-based partnership, a new hospital building, new arrangements for all the services) that they fail to see that they can and must make their conditions more livable for the long haul.

❖ **Seduction 5:** *No!* At a visceral level, when we first encounter this team, it is solidly engrossed in an ironclad rendition of *No!*. These nurse managers have many, many complaints about almost every aspect of their situation. One additional manifestation of this Seduction is that they strongly resist their CNE when she explicitly asks them to relinquish their grievances and change their perspectives.

❖ **Seduction 6:** *It's All About You.* Finally, although all the team members did not blame the CNE, a few of them did fault her for not seeing their plight and confirming that they were, in fact, powerless.

You may be developing an opinion as to which Seduction is primary. In this vignette, the main point is not the question of primacy. Individual team members are probably fixated on some Seductions more than others, but what is more important is the amplified concern that the team is creating as the Seductions spread and intensify among its members.

When Seductions spread, their intensity is likely to grow as group members share their individual renditions of the Seductions with each other. No matter which Seductions are most important to any particular leader, that leader will convincingly share a story and probably "infect" others who are listening. Remember that one of the qualities of the Seductions is that we like to enroll others in our potent versions of "the truth." When those around us are susceptible, they can be easily enticed, and soon they become champions of that Seduction, too.

WHAT'S NEXT FOR THIS TEAM?

What can this team do to reclaim its valor? After all, it is made up of accomplished professionals with good intentions, even if they are caught up in the drama and frenzy of having too much to do. We meet them when they have given up their power, their wisdom, and their long-term perspective.

Two actions could change things for this team. The first is that any individual team member could stop complaining and start hearing what the CNE is really saying. Alternatively, the CNE could stop talking and start listening and empathizing. One of the reasons for the team's resistance is that the CNE did not listen to what the team members believed were valid complaints.

Here's what happened:

> *The CNE changed her approach: She backed up and really listened to the group. Once she did, the group was able to calm down, let go of its collective struggle, and make a genuine shift toward valiant leadership. At that point, team members were able to allow other ideas in, and as they did, they reconsidered their justified,*

but unsustainable, positions. Eventually, they chose to curtail their endless trips around the mini-loop and Initiate *deeper levels of self-awareness as individuals and as a team. They were able to hear the CNE encouraging them to let go of their steadfast refusals to change and instead develop a workable strategy for what lay ahead.*

While the team members could not eliminate the priorities of their patients and the institution, they chose to reflect and reacquaint themselves with who they were and what was important to them as individuals and as a group (Illuminate). *After some soul-searching, they recognized their Seductions, and soon they saw that they actually could delegate more to others and say "no" from time to time. With the CNE's blessing, they developed specific follow-up plans (the Create part of Step 3:* Curate*) for themselves, and they also agreed to have monthly retreats for the foreseeable future. They wanted to meet more frequently to share their experiences and support one another, not just informally, but formally, too.*

WHAT ABOUT YOU?

What parts of this story do you identify with? For example, are there times when you wrap yourself in a justifiably righteous but destructive story that you "know" is true, even as it renders you powerless to improve your circumstances?

Notice that releasing yourself from a story like "I have too much to do" is especially difficult when your organization or society at large condones being ultra-busy. But no matter what your organization or society says, as a valiant leader, you can give yourself options other than just responding repeatedly and endlessly to situations that will take your all unless you intervene.

If you belong to a team, what lessons does this vignette offer you about how your team operates? For example:

❖ Does your team unwittingly perpetuate Seductions and tell (and perhaps even revel in) stories that are inaccurate? Initially in this vignette, the team's close connection fueled the contagion of the Seductions. But once the team was back on track and leading valiantly as a unit, these nurse leaders used that closeness and their mutual respect to move forward together. They developed plans to support one another so they could maintain their power, do their best work, and sustain themselves for the long haul.

❖ Think about whether your team's strength ever becomes a liability. If it does, what does this vignette teach you about how your team can lead valiantly when that happens?

❖ Notice that the team was engaged in the never-ending mini-loop of expediency and without an intervention by their CNE, they could have been caught in this futile behavior for a long time. No one on the team was able to step away and see the team's unproductive activities as the no-win strategies they were. Their insistence that they keep doing the same things made it very difficult for them to choose the Cycle of Leadership Valor and *Initiate* to find a better and more sustainable way forward.

- Are there times when you or others on your team go along with the group when pausing could help all of you in the long run?

- What do the lessons of this vignette tell you about how to *Initiate* and reflect even when the dynamics of the team seem unchangeable and unstoppable?

How to Stay Valiant When the Seductions Call Your Name

As we have seen in the vignettes and in Chapter 2, the Seductions drive all sorts of ill-serving leadership behaviors. When they remain unexamined, they can be the potent, destructive motivators behind our attitudes, beliefs, and actions. But as valiant leaders, we know that indulging in the Seductions is always a choice.

Here are some tips to consider when you are tempted by the Leadership Seductions.

GROUND YOURSELF

When a Seduction is about to take hold, try to maintain self-awareness as you face its temptation. If you can, pull back and remind yourself who you are and what you most want, not what you want in the moment. Consider the likely impact of your behavior.

Notice that Seductions usually gather steam when you are paying exclusive attention to consensus reality. For example, if a colleague tells you the team is going in a direction you "know" is "wrong," you may be tempted to caustically shoot down this observation because you know you are "right." If another team member adds her voice to the first supporting the "wrong" direction, you might resist even more, unless you have another equally important perspective to help you reframe your reaction. That perspective can be the firm foundation provided by your awareness of all Three Levels of Reality rather than the compelling but shortsighted temptation of only the here and now.

REFLECT

If you want to relinquish your Seductions but you can't quite do it, think about these questions:

- ❖ Why is it important to hold onto and act on this Seduction?
- ❖ What payoff will you get when you act on this Seduction?
- ❖ What assumptions are you making about this situation that may not be true?

❖ What is at stake if you don't relinquish this Seduction?

❖ What are the probable consequences of allowing this Seduction (or a combination of Seductions) to shape the way you lead in this situation?

❖ What would you do differently if you were not caught up in this Seduction?

❖ What will it take to let go of this Seduction?

TURN DOWN THE VOLUME

Yes, the Seduction is there, and yes, you feel its pull. You can acknowledge it and still divert your attention away from it and toward what you want at a deeper level. Will this be difficult? Yes. But the more you practice, the easier it will become.

TRY CURIOSITY INSTEAD OF JUDGMENT

When you are about to react, catch yourself and convert the statement you are about to make into a curious question. For example, if someone says, "You don't seem sincere," instead of immediately responding, "But I am sincere," think about why this person may be saying that. What is he seeing that you are not seeing? Then ask, "What am I doing that prompts you to say that?"

Remember That You May Not Be Aware of What Others Know

If you are enticed by a Seduction in reaction to what other people are saying or doing, remember that you do not know what factors may be influencing their behavior. Instead of becoming negative, impatient, and excessively focused on what's not working for you, see if you can explore what they know that you don't.

Consider Others' Intentions

When you don't know what other people intend by their actions and statements, try giving them the benefit of the doubt, even if their delivery or style is not what you prefer.

Let Your Symbol Anchor You

If you selected a symbol of yourself as a valiant leader (as suggested in Chapter 1), keep it visible. Look at it when a Leadership Seduction tempts you. Let your symbol anchor you in your possibility rather than your vulnerability.

FOCUS ON WHAT'S MOST IMPORTANT

Remember that your job is to lead valiantly, to perform to the best of your ability, and to learn as you go. Period.

VIGNETTE 7

INITIATING AND ILLUMINATING TRANSFORM A LEADER'S LIFE

This is the story of Elizabeth, who spent much of her professional life in senior leadership roles. She became a Chief Executive at the age of 30 and held top jobs in several healthcare organizations over the course of the next 2 decades. When she first took on her role as a senior healthcare leader, female executives were unusual. Like other women of her rank, Elizabeth felt that the standards for her performance were higher than they were for her male counterparts. To excel in their jobs and maintain their places on the corporate stage, Elizabeth and women like her believed they had to work exceedingly hard. Additionally, it seemed that society all but required them to be completely assured and have all the answers, all the time. Elizabeth, like other female leaders, internalized this belief, and she worked hard to demonstrate consistently strong, certain leadership.

For years, Elizabeth expended almost heroic levels of effort to orchestrate organizational success many times over, even when the odds were long. Along the way, she developed an "iron-clad" façade and a highly professional demeanor. Her veneer reflected her belief that she could not appear to be "weak" and that she had to maintain legitimacy and respect in the eyes of her male peers.

As Elizabeth progressed in her career, times changed. More women joined Elizabeth in the "C-suite," and there was more acceptance of leaders of both genders occasionally showing glimpses of their softer sides. As the expectations of female leaders slowly evolved, there was a bit more tolerance for them to be less steely.

Changing times were evident in Elizabeth's circles, too. But she was slow to adjust to this emerging reality. She was the first to say that the years of donning a protective cover had contributed to her success, but in the process, she had lost touch with much of her real self. Eventually, Elizabeth felt she no longer had access to who she was at a deeper level. While her carefully constructed professional front had served her for a time, its usefulness was becoming a thing of the past.

Elizabeth continued to manage her organization well enough, but she began to feel less fulfilled and engaged with her life. She was also losing appreciation for the rewards that leading her team had always given her. Her well-known sense of humor was failing her, too. Bits of feedback started to let her know that, at times, she sounded hollow and inauthentic to her peers. She saw that her impact on others was changing. Exactly how it was shifting eluded her, but she could see that who she had become was not who she wanted to be.

WHAT DO YOU NOTICE?

Although some of Elizabeth's story is an artifact of an earlier time, there are aspects of her evolution that are instructive for us today, no matter how old we are or what our corporate cultures dictate. Elizabeth offers us an example of a leader who needs to create a new and more vital version of herself as a leader and as a human being.

The first thing to notice is the truth of this quote from Dewitt Jones (1999): "If our patterns go unquestioned, they become our prisons." We can hardly blame Elizabeth for developing the strong sense of self that she felt she needed to survive and thrive in the world as it was. However, that world changed and as it did, Elizabeth's necessarily impenetrable identity became the prison that Jones describes. The pattern that once served her well is stifling her now.

As we read about Elizabeth, we can't help but see that she is transforming. It's possible that she had a long-standing vulnerability to the first Seduction, *I Am Right* (especially in manifesting "I must be the way I am"). But whether she would say she was inclined toward this Seduction or not, it is certain that being locked into this narrow version of who she is no longer serves her. "I must be me, in this form," doesn't resonate with Elizabeth any longer. It has lost its relevance and its appeal.

Notice that Elizabeth's growing discomfort with her identity renders one of her former stories obsolete as well. In the past, she told herself that she needed to work harder and be more steadfast than her male counterparts. We might say that her narrative was a calculated judgment rather than a distorted reality, so it was not *Storytelling*. But now, whether the story was ever a Seduction or not, it, too, is no longer relevant. She does not feel the need to over-compensate any longer.

Do you think Elizabeth has *Checked Out*? We know that she has lost touch with part of herself. But the information we have tells us that she is not completely checked out because she is aware of her feelings and the feedback her colleagues are giving her. If anything, we might say that Elizabeth is waking up. We know that she does not want to continue on the path she's on precisely because she does not want to be checked out.

WHAT WAS NEXT FOR ELIZABETH?

We can see that Elizabeth sacrificed a lot of herself to conform professionally, but, over time, this way of coping exacted too great a cost: the loss of a deep and abiding connection with herself. Here's what she did next.

> *Elizabeth was becoming aware of the "prison" that her life and her beliefs had become. She felt no need to be hard on herself about these emerging truths, but she was compelled to find her way back to her true spirit as a human being and as a leader. Whether she had once been a valiant leader did not concern her; she wanted to update her life and her leadership style now. And she was willing to do what it took to make it happen.*

Elizabeth was eager to choose the Cycle of Leadership Valor, and she gladly took the first step, Initiate. *She knew her real work would come with the second step,* Illuminate. *In taking that step, she realized she had become so influenced—and driven—by the era she lived in (a form of consensus reality) that her view of its imperatives had the upper hand in her life for many, many years. She knew she had much to relearn about her essence, or who she was at her core, and she was also eager to update her aspirations and her dreams. By choosing Leadership Valor and engaging in the first and second steps, Elizabeth was on her way to reclaiming a renewed version of herself as a person and as a valiant leader.*

WHAT ABOUT YOU?

Elizabeth's circumstances provide a vivid example of a way of leading that no longer fits. While there is little doubt that Elizabeth does not think of her ingrained responses to her culture as repeatedly invoking the mini-loop of expediency, we see that, in fact, that's what she did for many years. As we leave Elizabeth's journey, think about whether and how aspects of her story relate to yours by considering the following questions:

❖ Are there ways in which your own leadership style no longer suits you? Perhaps it once did, but now, do you also invoke the mini-loop over and over again out of habit?

❖ Are there ways in which you, too, lead just as you always have, even though those ways confine you unnecessarily?

If you answer yes to either of these questions, consider how you will feel if this same thing is true next year and the year after that. If you are prompted to renew your leadership style as Elizabeth did, what will your first steps be?

Initiating and *Illuminating*

As you have seen in many of the stories and vignettes so far, the first steps on the Cycle of Leadership Valor are often the hardest. Here are some tips that can help you stay conscious and flexible.

Tips for Choosing Step 1: *Initiate*

Choosing Leadership Valor can be more than difficult when you feel you "must" react quickly and routinely, even when the circumstances warrant a thoughtful and deliberate response. If you are attracted by the pull of the mini-loop of expediency even when it's not appropriate, try these ideas to help you *Initiate* instead.

Buy Time

When you are tempted to react immediately even though you know you should step back and reflect, give yourself a few minutes.

Remember that there's almost never a circumstance that you have to address right now. Even if you are just working through an issue in your head, you can still counsel yourself by saying, "I need to take a few minutes. Before I do anything, I am going to think about this."

BREATHE DEEPLY

This is the least you can do for yourself. It's simple, and it works.

REMEMBER THAT EMOTIONAL "FLOODING" IS REAL

There are times when our emotions are so powerful that they take over our limbic systems. In these moments it is almost biologically impossible for human beings to respond thoughtfully versus reactively. Honor your humanity, realize that your strong emotions are natural, and give yourself some time to settle down before you act.

DEVELOP YOUR OBSERVER SELF

What is the observer self? It is the capacity we have to "see" ourselves. Remember that choosing to *Initiate* is electing to expand self-awareness. One way we can achieve greater self-awareness is by developing the ability to observe ourselves as we act and as we speak. We can do what we're doing and also be aware of what we're doing.

It might help to think about this capacity as standing on a balcony and overlooking the action—and yourself—on the main floor. You can "take yourself" to this balcony and learn from what you see about yourself and the situation and people around you. Ronald

Heifetz and Martin Linsky (2002) use the balcony metaphor because being there provides a different perspective from being an "actor" on the main stage. As noted in Chapter 3, an additional perspective is what we're after as valiant leaders. It is another vantage point that's equally valid yet differs substantially from what we see in the thick of the action of leadership.

TIPS FOR CHOOSING STEP 2: *ILLUMINATE*

After you have chosen to *Initiate* rather than react, you can use these tips to move into and through Step 2: *Illuminate*. Remembering what is most important by considering your Three Levels of Reality can ground you like nothing else. Similarly, uncovering the Seductions that may be affecting you can restore you to your better, more valiant way of leading.

REMEMBER THAT YOU ARE MORE THAN YOUR CIRCUMSTANCES

You don't have to react immediately to every situation that appears to be urgent—usually falsely. Instead, you can opt for self-awareness and then take the next step, *Illuminate*. Both will help you rise above your circumstances. Being in touch and staying in touch with the fullest version of who you are and what you most want will assist you in staying clear on your direction. Leading valiantly is not always easy, but your chances of success are enhanced when you have the fullest version of your integrity to keep you focused.

Listen—To Others and to Yourself

Elizabeth's story in Vignette 7 reminds us of the value of being awake to ourselves. If Elizabeth had not heeded her growing discomfort and the feedback others gave her, she might have continued to feel demoralized for a long time. She might not have been alert enough to choose Leadership Valor, deeply engage with *Illuminating*, and be on solid footing as she regained her vitality and her focus.

Slow Down

Elizabeth was getting ready to shed an old identity. That may or may not be true for you. Whether it is or not, as a busy leader, you can still experience the powerful compulsion to simply move from situation to resolution and back again. Working that expedient mini-loop is appropriate as long as you have the expertise and it's the right thing to do. But if you question whether that's true, or if you just want to take a few minutes to reflect on what's happening, there is great benefit in just slowing down.

VIGNETTE 8
CURATING AT ITS BEST

Angela had been a chief executive officer for several years, and be-fore that, she was a chief nursing officer in a large regional health-care organization. Angela was a woman of great presence. She knew who she was, what she stood for, and what she wanted her team and their health system to do for their patients.

One of Angela's most significant qualities was that she was keenly aware of her personal power and her effect on other people. For example, she realized that when she spoke, even if she was only presenting an opinion, those listening to her often thought she was giving them direction. She also knew that people could be reluctant to disagree or even offer additional perspectives when she was present.

Angela could have been distressed by this fact because it did not match with her belief that better decisions are made when there are multiple points of view to evaluate. This and other examples of Angela's considerable impact could have tempted her to use her power inappropriately. She could have easily influenced, and even manipulated, some of the other leaders and the staff so they would do what she wanted them to do. But Angela didn't make the choice to manipulate. While she very much wanted the staff to provide excellent patient care, she wanted them to do it because they were dedicated professionals who believed in and excelled at what they were doing. She wanted them to be committed to the organization's mission, and she wanted their own personal beliefs and professional standards to make that vision come alive. She wanted them to be aware of and fulfill their own wishes to create a thriving organization and healthier patients. In other words, she wanted her colleagues to be valiant leaders in their own right.

So, while Angela could have been excessively calculating and even unethical, she chose instead to take a different route to sustainable, integrity-based leadership. She demonstrated this commitment in many ways including this ordinary, everyday example: She was quite thoughtful about which meetings she attended. There were times when she consciously chose to sit meetings out even though some expected her to participate and others simply wanted her to be there. She did this so that the people in the meeting took ownership, spoke freely, and made decisions on their own.

When she did attend meetings, there were occasions when she explicitly stated her role in being there. Certainly, when Angela attended as the CEO who was making final decisions, she didn't need to explicitly say so, because people assumed that was her function. But when her presence did require clarification, she provided it. For example, if she was attending as a participant like all the other participants, she articulated that role. Angela's goal was to intentionally create environments in which her function was clear, others were empowered, and robust dialogue occurred whether she was present or not.

WHAT DO YOU NOTICE?

Angela demonstrates her personal version of valiant leadership in several ways:

❖ She could not be this strategic about her choices were she not self-aware and practiced. It is apparent that Angela has taken the time to reflect and to develop her own form of powerful, valiant leadership.

❖ Angela could easily be taken in by *I Am Right*, including its variations: "I am great," and "Other people 'worship' me so of course I'm right." But instead, she is willing to forego some of the adulation that could surely be hers.

❖ Angela could be stuck in a story about how much power and influence she wields, and she could easily act it out. Notice, however, that if there is such a story, it is not a Seduction, because she consciously manages its potential impact on the way she leads. She does not overplay her power nor does she use it for ill-gotten gain.

❖ Angela is firmly aware of and anchored in her Three Levels of Reality. She knows what is happening, who she is, and what she wants.

❖ Angela consciously practices Step 3 on a regular basis. She *Curates* her leadership with conscious intention. She makes deliberate choices about how to lead and how to influence people. She knows she will have an effect on those around her, so she is measured when exercising her influence, rather than denying that it exists. She is selective about the meetings she attends, and, when necessary, she explains her role. She not only clarifies these choices in her own mind; she also makes them explicit when needed.

WHAT ABOUT YOU?

You do not have to be a powerful CEO who is masterfully self-aware to relate to the lessons of Angela's story. And, you do not have to be a seasoned, experienced leader like Angela to lead valiantly. All leaders can exhibit valor, regardless of their stage of development as leaders.

A novice leader is likely to need specific guidelines to lead successfully and may also have less confidence than Angela does. There is nothing wrong with this state of leadership. In fact, there is everything right with it. It takes practice, patience, and willingness to develop any skill to the exemplary level displayed by Angela. She and everyone like her started as a newer leader. Angela developed her finesse by exercising choice, by developing her awareness, by consciously choosing to practice the skills and ways of being that now make her so effective, and by learning from her experiences.

No matter your level of leadership experience, you can develop your own version of expertise and polish as a valiant leader. Here are some questions and perspectives to consider as you do that:

- ❖ Are there aspects of Angela's way of leading that are similar to your own? If so, what are they?

- ❖ Does Angela's version of valiant leadership inspire you to think and act differently? If so, in what ways?

- ❖ Are you conscious of the roles you play as you go through your day?

Notice that Angela was clear that she did not have the same role in every context, even though her job title was always CEO. In some meetings, she was just a participant, in some she was the chief decision maker, and in others she declined to participate at all.

Angela demonstrates a best practice for valiant leaders. She consciously determines her role before going into certain settings. You can do this, too. You can ask yourself what role you are expected to play—and what role you think you should play—in a given situation. If it is to manage, to lead, and to inspire, how can you fulfill those roles valiantly?

If you have difficulty identifying the part you play in different settings, think instead about your "voice," or even your reason for being, in those situations. For instance, your purpose could be to function in some of the following ways:

- ❖ To provide information, guidance, counsel, or advice

- ❖ To be listened to and to be heard

❖ To listen and to hear others

❖ To empathize

❖ To supervise

❖ To teach

❖ To mentor or coach

❖ To problem solve

❖ To brainstorm

❖ To fulfill other equally valid functions

If you aren't sure which roles you play, take notice of them as you go through your day. Also notice whether you unconsciously usurp other people's roles.

If more role clarity can help you lead with more intention and valor, what will you do to practice and develop this skill?

CREATING AND CALIBRATING WHEN THE STAKES ARE HIGH

Roger was one of the senior staff leaders in a not-for-profit organization with a broad geographic reach, many services, and a large group of stakeholders. The stakeholders were all invested in the business that was conducted and the way policies and procedures were envisioned and implemented. While no one argued about the significance of this organization's work on behalf of quality healthcare, some said that its many volunteer leaders were focused more on maintaining their own power than on attending to the needs of the organization and the community it served.

Despite the politics inherent in an environment like this, Roger and his staff peers knew something had to be done to ensure the institution's long-term viability. They feared for its very survival unless it changed its approach to its business. They acknowledged that tackling this challenge would not be easy. Yet he and his team had studied the data, and they were convinced that the numbers accurately projected a bleak financial picture unless major change occurred. So they developed several viable scenarios for its future and committed to doing what it took to improve the organization's prospects for survival. But how would they manage to turn such a complicated and entrenched entity around?

How indeed. They knew this would take long-term, committed, and valiant leadership on the part of each member of the team and the team as a whole. They would need to bring the best of their fortitude to each encounter to get the job done. In addition, they would need to bring in the board's officers to define and champion the vision and lead the dialogue because without them, forward motion would be impossible. They recognized that they would have to stand up to the factions that wanted to maintain the status quo, and that they also had to communicate clearly, repeatedly, and con-sistently. Stakeholders removed from the central operations of the organization would not immediately understand the compelling need for change, but even so, their buy-in would be essential.

The team members would also have to define what success for this initiative would look like. Would it be gaining approval for every element of their proposed changes? Were they willing to accept some progress rather than achieving everything?

WHAT DO YOU NOTICE?

Roger and his colleagues are very clear on their mission, their direction, and the depth of their commitment. We can imagine that they have taken time, perhaps even a great deal of time, to step away from their routines in order to focus on this massive project and its enormous consequences. Their commitment and their thoughtful questions tell us that they have collectively chosen to lead valiantly. We can see that they have taken the first step: They have *Initiated* a reflective process to take on this daunting task.

They also engaged deeply in the work of Step 2: *Illuminate.* Roger and his staff colleagues have the data they need to know exactly where the organization stands (consensus reality). They also have clarity about the organization's reason for being (essence reality) and viable scenarios that could secure its long-term future (dreaming reality). In addition, they know what they want in the immediate future. Their concern about the organization's welfare fuels their very strong commitment to do what it takes so it can survive (another aspect of dreaming reality).

WHAT WAS NEXT FOR ROGER AND HIS TEAM?

Because they had engaged deeply with Steps 1 and 2, Roger and his colleagues were ready to take these next steps:

Committed as they were, the members of Roger's team knew they had an enormous challenge on their hands. They devoted many months to engaging the officers of the board in planning sessions, creating a long-term vision for the organization, and preparing for the early phases of its implementation. They also spent a great deal of time speaking with other formal stakeholders, talking with the numerous groups that were involved, and conducting count-less informal dialogues with the many powerful people connected to this enterprise. All the while, they maintained their focus on ensuring the organization's existence and their plans for achieving this overarching goal.

However, as they engaged with their many constituents, they found that they had to adjust and even re-create parts of their plans again and again. Although some of the changes caused them self-described "heartburn," they rigorously screened each proposed change by asking whether making it would enhance or harm the initiative and the long-term potential of the organization. They were not willing to make changes that would seriously disrupt their efforts or the organization's ability to fulfill its important mission.

Finally, a year later and after a great deal of back and forth with the many different constituents who were involved, Roger and the rest of the team were ready to present the plan to the large and disparate group of individuals that governed the whole of the or-ganization. Not surprisingly, they held many pre-meetings before the day of the vote. In those meetings before the meeting, some "horse-trading" occurred, and some parts of the plan were adjusted yet again.

In the end, Roger and the other senior staff members were quite happy with the results of the vote: Most, but not all, aspects of their "final" plan were adopted. As these leaders reflected on their journey, they were visibly relieved. Roger remarked that they felt they had "turned the Titanic around." Neither Roger nor his team was concerned that they had adjusted strategies and changed plans along the way, because they had been diligent about vetting the shifts, even at the eleventh hour. Each change had to pass through the lens of their commitment to their core purpose: to ensure the organization's survival so it could continue to perform its vital function on behalf of patients.

The team was also not concerned that the voting representatives had not adopted all of their recommendations. They felt that the rest of the changes would come in due time. They believed they had been "successful enough" for the organization to have a good chance of surviving well into the coming years. They breathed a collective sigh of relief when they deemed the effort "complete," even though there would be many ramifications of the changes for many months, and perhaps years, to come.

WHAT ABOUT YOU?

You may not be a senior leader in a complex healthcare organization with as many tentacles as Roger's. But your world is just as vital, and the need for creating workable leadership plans and strategies is just as important. The story of Roger's team illustrates the power of valiant leadership at the team and individual levels, and the importance of calibration, especially when a lack of flexibility will almost certainly damage or destroy any important undertaking.

Consider these questions as you apply Roger's experience to your own leadership.

- ❖ When you are creating a plan to approach an opportunity or a problem, how clear are you on the outcome you want to achieve?

- ❖ When you have been thoughtful about the strategy you want to use in a situation, how willing are you to adjust it when those around you tell you your plan, as it is, won't work?

- ❖ How do you react when you encounter resistance to your vision and your plans?

- ❖ What is your reaction when the cooperation you need to succeed is slow to take hold?

- ❖ If your stakeholders don't understand an imperative because they are not familiar with the details, what do you do?

- ❖ When you are orchestrating a change, what is the effect of your messages about the need for change? If your messages don't have the impact you want, what can you do to adapt, or calibrate, the way you communicate so others can better absorb what you want them to know?

- ❖ How willing are you to accept "enough" success if accomplishing everything is not possible? If you are willing to accept "enough" instead of all the success that's conceivable, how will you define "enough"?

EXPANDING YOUR CAPACITY TO CALIBRATE

Why calibrate? Isn't there something to be said for knowing your leadership stance and sticking with it? Yes, certainly. But not in every case. The trick is to discern when to stay with a plan or style of leading and when to change it. Here are some ways to appreciate the importance of calibration as a component of leading valiantly and deepen your capacity to calibrate.

PERSPECTIVES ABOUT CALIBRATION

Calibration is about evolving and adjusting as you go along. All living things must self-correct to stay alive and to grow. Here are some additional benefits of expanding your capacity to calibrate:

❖ There is almost always more than one right answer or approach to a situation; calibrating allows you to access other right answers in addition to the one you chose originally.

❖ Think about calibration as a skillset that permits you to tweak or surrender a position that will not work or does not serve you.

❖ Knowing when and how to calibrate permits you to let go of excessive attachments of all kinds, including but not limited to the Leadership Seductions.

❖ One component of calibration is the ability to know and be skillful about when to emphasize *yin* and when to emphasize *yang*. Yin and yang are opposites in nature that can't exist without each other. They are always shifting and, ideally, they maintain overall balance as they do. One (yin) is about yielding, and the other (yang) is about asserting. Although yin is associated with the feminine and yang with the masculine, we all have both types of these opposing but complementary forces within us. We want to be capable of calibrating by yielding when called for and being assertive when that's a better choice.

TIPS FOR CALIBRATING

Here are some tips that can enhance your skill with calibration.

INCREASE FLEXIBILITY

What do you do to keep yourself physically flexible? What helps you remain agile in other facets of your life? How can you use these and similar skills to enhance your capacity to calibrate when you choose to?

SEEK NOVELTY

Deliberately put yourself in situations that are new and challenging. To get really good at responding well in brand-new circumstances, take an improvisation class.

DISTINGUISH BETWEEN SUBSTANCE AND STYLE

When you need to calibrate, identify what type of adjustment you need to make. Is it a shift in substance (what you stand for or what you are doing), or is it a shift in style (the way you are doing it), or is it both?

ASK YOURSELF QUESTIONS

When you're not sure if it's wise to calibrate, ask yourself these questions:

❖ Is your strategy working?

❖ Are there parts of your plan that are not acceptable to others?

    • If so, what are they, and do you want to change them?

- If you don't want to change them, are you thinking that you are right and others are wrong? If so, consider whether the first Seduction (*I Am Right*) is influencing you in ways that don't serve you in this situation.

RECALL YOUR VISION

If you know you need to adjust but are reluctant, remember your vision for yourself as a valiant leader. Will calibrating take you closer to or further away from realizing that vision?

IMAGINE THE WORST POSSIBLE OUTCOME

If you are afraid to change your plan but think you should, imagine the worst outcome that could occur if you try something new and the results are disappointing. Is it worth doing anyway?

THINK ABOUT CALIBRATION IN ADVANCE

If you anticipate the need to be flexible but don't want to do it, think through some possible events that could prompt or "force" you to calibrate. Then ask:

❖ How will you react? Will you buy time, will you acquiesce, or will you resist?

❖ Will you, in fact, move in a different direction?

If the circumstance you are contemplating is important, consider likely scenarios and then devise plans for each so you know what to do if the need to change direction materializes.

USE THE CYCLE AND THE STEPS TO CHALLENGE UNPRODUCTIVE TENDENCIES

Notice your capacity to adjust your leadership as you go through any given day on the job. See if any patterns emerge. If you find you aren't willing to "flex" in a lot of circumstances that would benefit from it, *Initiate* the Cycle of Leadership Valor.

When you move along to *Illuminate,* reflect on your reluctance. See if there are common threads in the situations in which you resist calibrating. Recall your core and your dream, too. Think about the Seductions and whether they are contributing to a pattern of inflexibility.

Then come back to *Curate* and put it all together by considering:

❖ What does your review of the first two steps tell you about your unwillingness to bend when doing so would yield a better outcome?

❖ Even if you are uncomfortable at first, are you willing to try calibration when it will move you closer to the outcomes you seek?

VIGNETTE 10
THE VALUE OF
INTEGRATING

In Vignette 9, "Creating and Calibrating When the Stakes Are High," Roger and his team orchestrated a complicated organizational shift that many considered to be transformational. Although implementing the many changes adopted by the organization would take months, if not years, Roger was intent on taking some time to reflect and Integrate *(Step 4) while the experience was fresh.*

Roger was a seasoned leader, but he had never before had the opportunity, or the compelling need, to lead such a massive turnaround effort. Meeting this challenge had consumed well over a year, and it had tested his resolve on many occasions. He was certain there was much to learn from his experience, and he didn't want to focus on only what worked. Although he was eager to savor the wins he and the team had facilitated, he also wanted to think critically about what didn't go as well as he had hoped.

Roger thought about his experience on and off for the next month, and he uncovered these key insights.

The reward for resisting Seductions. *In such a highly charged political environment, Roger had encountered daily temptations to give in to the Seductions. Sometimes all of them seemed to beckon him. Many vocal, pessimistic naysayers had stood in his way. In the face of so much negativity and resistance, it would have been easy for Roger to adopt, and stick with, verbiage and a tone that conveyed certainty that he was "right." But he knew this was a Seduction and that any satisfaction he gleaned from indulging it would be shortsighted. He also knew that cultivating a sentiment of collective righteousness and spreading it to others on the team would be counterproductive.*

Storytelling, *too, could have become quite a pastime for him and the other members of the team. It would have been all too easy for them to exaggerate the ignorance of other stakeholders who, by definition, had less information and fewer facts. It would have been even easier to devalue their perspectives. But neither the team members nor Roger did much of that: They didn't have time, and more importantly, they didn't have the will. Instead, they focused on getting the job done.*

So, one of the lasting lessons Roger took with him is that no matter how powerful the pull of Seductions in the moment, there is always more important work to do. For him, the Seductions lost a lot of their attraction when he stayed focused on what was important rather than what was tempting.

The importance of balance. *Roger also thought about how he and the team kept their commitment alive and their energy fresh over such a long period of time. While they all worked hard, and they often worked long hours, they also took at least some weekends* *off. Roger had been of two minds about this during the intense period that lasted many, many months. As the team's leader, he needed to guide their work and meet with their many constituents. But he also felt it was important to model a somewhat sustainable work schedule. The idea of balance was not difficult for Roger because he genuinely wanted to take care of himself. Still, upon reflection, he hadn't done as well as he wanted with balancing his multiple commitments. He had a lifelong passion for basketball, but he had not played much in the past year. As he reflected, he realized that his lack of exercise led to his increasingly frequent backaches. Regrettably, he had also gained a few pounds, so he vowed to get back on the court as soon as possible.*

The satisfaction of sharing the limelight. *Roger was very proud of what his team accomplished, and he thought about times in the past when he would have wanted more individual credit for this kind of success. He thought a bit about his age, and he concluded that he must be older and wiser because it genuinely gratified him to think about his role in mentoring the younger leaders. Their work was truly exceptional, and it contributed substantially to the team's eventual success. He wasn't sure he completely liked being the "older and wiser" guide, but he did like having the wisdom and confidence to let others have their well-earned share of the glory.*

An appreciation for the right level of calibration. *Roger contemplated how much success was enough success. He revisited the process involved in getting to a set of resolutions that was acceptable to all concerned. Defining success, and then redefining it frequently during their many negotiations, had demanded a lot of time and attention from him, the staff team, and the board leaders who backed the effort. In numerous meetings, they had examined* *changes that could have eased eventual passage while also questioning whether the changes would cost the organization too much in exchange.*

He decided that one of his key take-aways was that although calibration was a critical element of success for a complex venture like this, he and his colleagues were wise to stay "on their toes" so they wouldn't give too much. It would have been a serious mistake to accommodate too many changes and in doing so, lose their integrity and, potentially, the organization's main reason for being. Dramatic as this sounded, this was a real lesson and an important one for Roger to Integrate.

The inspiration for sustaining valiant leadership. *Roger respected the fine points of calibration, and he was glad to have seen its advantages as well as its potential limitations. He thought a lot about the courage, grit, and true valor that the team displayed. Every day, they had demonstrated that they were in it to win it. Even though they had to continually re-examine what succeeding really meant, there was no doubt that this team was "all in." Together and separately, they had leveraged their skills and their belief in the organization and in themselves as leaders. They had each exhibited valor in their own ways, on their own terms, but they had done so in concert with one another and in service of achieving their collective goal of saving the organization.*

WHAT DO YOU NOTICE?

While few of us lead massive, complex organizations or transformational change initiatives of the sort that Roger and his colleagues handled, we can still learn from the way Roger models *Integrating*. We can see that he reflects on not just his successes, but also on aspects of the experience of which he was less proud. Notice that far from retreating to a mountain top, Roger unearths and *Integrates* what he learns by being committed to simply reflecting on and off for a few weeks.

You can see some of what Roger gained from *Integrating*, such as a solid appreciation for the splendid work of his protégés, and his keen awareness of the potential power of the Seductions and a proven way to elude them. He also fully acknowledged the toll his lack of exercise took on his body.

WHAT WAS NEXT FOR ROGER?

After participating in and witnessing this transformative—and valiant—leadership journey, Roger felt genuinely humbled and truly inspired. As he looked forward, he thought about how he would apply what he had learned from this deeply satisfying experience:

> *In the future, if he were to become tempted by a Seduction or think that something difficult couldn't be done, Roger knew that he could find and sustain his courage by tapping into the memory of the enormous success he and his colleagues orchestrated.*

He felt certain that the long-term commitment he and his team made to changing the trajectory of their organization would benefit the healthcare field and their enterprise for a long time to come. Due to the nature of his organization's work, Roger knew that its challenges would not subside. Yet he also knew that the success he and his team had achieved would buoy them for many months and years to come.

WHAT ABOUT YOU?

Roger was deliberate about "harvesting" the learning from the significant experience he and his team members had. What can you learn from Roger's experience with *Integrating*? Here are some ways to leverage his approach so it is meaningful to you:

❖ When you think about how committed Roger is to *Integrating,* ask yourself how often you deliberately take the time to reflect on small moments, routine events, or big initiatives in your own leadership life.

❖ While we don't have the details about when and where Roger did the work of *Integrating,* we have enough information to know that he didn't set up anything elaborate to enhance his integration. You, too, can do something simple to *Integrate.* It can be as straightforward as thinking about the day you just had and asking yourself what went well and what didn't. You can consider what you would do differently the next time, and you can also take a few minutes to appreciate the efforts of those around you.

❖ Notice how Roger thinks about success. He considers how much success was enough, and the process he, the team, and the board leaders used to define success—and then redefine it—when the dialogue changed and new information and demands emerged.

❖ Notice the valor Roger shows in approaching integration. Even in the glow of the huge win he and his team facilitated, he doesn't just examine their triumphs—or his own. Instead, he looks at his own leadership critically and when he doesn't like what he sees, he vows to change it.

LEADING VALIANTLY WITH A SINGLE WORD

Some years ago, Rowena was a young staff nurse who worked on a unit where her peers were leaving in droves. Rowena believed that several factors contributed to the mass exodus of her fellow nurses:

❖ *Their manager, Maya, was "frightening," "extremely critical," and their "worst nightmare."*

❖ *The director that Maya reported to was "not good."*

❖ *The hospital was implementing a new, comprehensive technology project. It had many wrinkles that were causing a lot of stress for the physicians, the staff, the managers, and the floor nurses.*

Rowena wanted this job for many reasons, both personal and professional, so she was doing her best to stay despite the difficulties. But one day, in front of the other nurses on her unit, Maya asked her to manipulate a feature of the new system in a way that she felt could compromise patient care. Maya's request seriously upset Rowena. In addition to worrying about the potential adverse effect on patients, Rowena was troubled because she felt that doing what Maya asked would be unethical, too.

Rowena felt her heart pounding in her chest, but she had to do what was right: She took a deep breath and said "no" to her boss. She briefly explained why she was declining, and she attempted to give her reasons in a straightforward and respectful manner.

Later, as she recounted the story, Rowena said she felt like time stopped when Maya asked her to do this. She was very frightened (in her words, "terrified") for what felt like several long moments between Maya's request and her eventual refusal. As Rowena said "no" and offered her reasons, Maya flinched and gave her a stern look of disapproval. But she said nothing as she turned away and approached another nurse who didn't hesitate to say "yes."

For the next couple of days Rowena waited for "the other shoe to drop." But nothing happened. She was surprised that there were no immediate consequences, and, in fact, there was no penalty at all. Through the hospital grapevine, it didn't take long for the Chief Nursing Officer (CNO) to find out about Rowena's act of courage. When she did, she came to Rowena's floor and requested to speak with her privately. She asked her what happened and after listening carefully to Rowena's response, the CNO praised her for her brave decision to say "no" and stand up for patient safety and her view of ethical nursing practice.

She then asked Rowena if she would like to take part in a special committee that was charged with creating better patient experiences through improved cross-departmental communication. Rowena was thrilled and said "yes" immediately. But at the same time, she was also apprehensive because she believed that participating with this group required knowledge and experience she didn't have.

Rowena felt very good about standing by her convictions, especially after being sought out and praised by the CNO, even though she had been "scared to death." The CNO's acknowledgment of her courage—and her valor—were so encouraging that Rowena soon overcame her concern about her ability to fully participate in the committee. She went on to actively contribute to its work, right along with other professionals who were far more senior than she.

WHAT DO YOU NOTICE?

Rowena serves as an inspiring example of valiant leadership. She had no information about leading valiantly per se, nor did she have any previous leadership experience to show her the way. She also didn't have time to talk with anyone else before she made her decision to refuse her boss's directive.

We can all learn from examining Rowena's simple yet profound choice to lead valiantly with just one word: "No." Here are a few observations about her courageous leadership when retribution from her boss seemed possible or even likely:

❖ Rowena's self-awareness gave her immediate access to her innate sense of right and wrong, her professional training, and her belief in herself, even in the face of potentially negative consequences.

❖ Despite her age and her lack of leadership experience, Rowena was willing to say "no" to a frightening and powerful boss. She demonstrated exceptional (and exceptionally valiant) leadership in that moment. Standing up to a boss is more than difficult for many of us; doing so at Rowena's stage of life and professional development is truly extraordinary.

❖ Rowena was asked to do something that she felt was unethical and could potentially compromise patient care. Understandably, she was afraid of the consequences when she contemplated responding with either "yes" or "no." She felt even more emotional when she decided to say "no": She was "terrified" and her "heart pounded," but she proceeded anyway. In that moment, Rowena learned something very important about bold leadership: She could be afraid *and* do the right thing at the same time.

❖ Rowena stood by her beliefs, and she communicated them clearly and directly. Even as she refused her boss, she did everything she could to maintain her composure, speak respectfully, and state her reasons in a straightforward way.

❖ Although Rowena's moment of decision led to a wonderful acknowledgement by the CNO, this kind of outcome was not even imaginable when she made her choice. In fact, she acted on her beliefs even though she was almost certain her powerful supervisor would react negatively.

WHAT WAS NEXT FOR ROWENA?

As she tells the story many years later, this series of incidents was pivotal in establishing the trajectory of Rowena's long and distinguished career. She became a principled leader who is admired for her ethical, unambiguous positions and her outstanding ability to guide and mentor others.

WHAT ABOUT YOU?

Are there circumstances in your leadership life that would be aided by greater clarity, or people who would benefit from hearing a more distinct "yes" or "no" from you? If so, how can your knowledge of leading valiantly help you be clearer in those circumstances?

As you reflect on Rowena's remarkable story, recall times in your life when you have done something that required you to summon a great deal of strength and courage. Think about one or two examples and pick the one that is most memorable. Recall what happened. See if you can remember the feelings you had as you acted, even in the face of unknown and possibly negative consequences.

❖ What difference did your actions make?

❖ What did you learn from this incident?

❖ What do you notice and how do you feel as you look back on this important moment in your life?

❖ Are there any aspects of this experience that you think of as gifts? If so, what are they?

❖ What does this incident and your reaction to it tell you about your capacity to lead valiantly?

Questions, Answers, and Practices

The collection of Vignettes and Perspectives and Tips in Part II demonstrates just some of many ways to lead valiantly. Here are several questions and answers that can take you even further in your understanding of how to lead with valor in your own way.

Questions and Answers About Leading Valiantly

Do I have to be a seasoned, experienced leader to be valiant?

Absolutely not. You can exhibit valor regardless of your stage of development as a leader. If you are a "novice," as described in the opening of Chapter 4, you may want to adhere to the specific guidelines offered by the steps, and you may not be as confident as those who are more experienced. These realities are normal aspects of learning anything new, and there is nothing wrong with these dynamics. In fact, there is much that is right about them, as noted in Vignette 11 and as you will discover when we explore mastering Leadership Valor in Chapter 6.

How does valiant leadership relate to feeling victimized?

Leading with valor allows you to uncover your innate personal power instead of feeling and acting like a victim. Valiant leadership is not about creating courage that you don't already have. It is about finding and releasing the courage that is already within you.

Am I less valiant if I forget and jump too quickly into the mini-loop of expediency or find myself embroiled in Seductions?

No. You are human. While this sounds obvious enough, it's easy to overlook this fact when you notice that your first approach to a situation does not represent you at your best. Sometimes even the most valiant leaders act impulsively, much to their later regret. If this happens to you, reflect on what happened and what you learned. Even more importantly: Forgive yourself, self-correct, and move on.

What is my responsibility to other people when I am committed to leading valiantly?

In addition to paying attention to your own development as a valiant leader, you can support and nurture valor in others. When you want to motivate others in this way, remember to manage your stories about them and with them. Focus on your beliefs about their accomplishments or their potential rather than heeding other filters that may negatively color how you relate to them. In other words, leave your baggage about them at the door. For more perspectives about leading valiantly with others, please see the "Mastery and Others" section in Chapter 6.

Ways to Practice Leading Valiantly

The following section offers a broad array of practices that you can use to develop your skill and capacity to lead more courageously. Pick those that resonate with you. If needed, adjust them so they precisely fit you and your preferences.

Write to Your Future Self

If you want to lead in a bolder way but can't find the gumption to do it, write yourself a letter. Imagine that you are an older and wiser version of yourself, at least 5, 10, or 15 years older than you are now. Picture yourself then as if you are speaking to yourself now, through the years via the words on the page. What would this wiser version of you say to help the current you lead in a bolder way?

Commit to Daily Practice

To strengthen your valor, commit to practicing in some way every day. Daily practice helps all of us stay awake and up-to-date with who we are and what is happening around us. Here are some examples of the small but meaningful commitments you can make:

❖ Commit to taking a single action or making a statement that you consider "valor worthy" every day, starting today. It can be small or large. It could be as simple as deciding to speak up in a meeting. It does not have to be the same thing every day— just do *something* every day.

❖ Think about activities that bring out the best in you. Do at least one of those today.

❖ Think about what inspires you. Reflect on or do that today.

❖ Think about what keeps you centered and fresh. Do that today, too.

MAKE A DEAL WITH YOURSELF

Create a valor-related contract or agreement with yourself. Make the goals achievable and include something that you will do to sustain yourself as a valiant and courageous leader every day. For ideas, start with your responses to the preceding "Commit to Daily Practice" section.

KEEP YOUR VISION NEARBY AND REFRESHED

If you developed a vision of yourself as a valiant leader as suggested in Chapter 1, keep it handy. Make notes about successes that tell you that your vision is real and achievable. Adjust and update your vision as circumstances change. Keeping it alive in a tangible way increases the chances that you will keep it alive inside yourself, too.

Focus on the Benefits and Embrace Your Success…Realistically

Remind yourself of the outcomes you visualized as part of being a valiant leader. Remember what being a valiant leader will allow you to do and how your work will benefit you and others.

As you think about your potential achievements, be realistic. Leadership success is usually gradual, and most of us follow a trajectory that is anything but a straight line up.

Reflect

Integrate your day. Get into the habit of thinking about it from start to finish. What went well? What didn't go so well? What will you do differently the next time?

Understand and Manage Your Own Resistance

Resistance is a normal part of being human, and your work as a valiant leader is to get to the bottom of it, learn what you need to, and address it so you can move on. To manage your own resistance, be sure you are aware of your usual ways of displaying it. They could include:

❖ Being confused

❖ Saying "no" a lot

❖ Denying what you don't want to know, do, hear, or see

❖ Feeling and saying "I don't know" frequently

❖ Checking out (when excessive, this is the third Seduction)

❖ Engaging with the other Seductions even when you know that it's counterproductive

Then, familiarize yourself with these antidotes for resistance:

❖ Choose to *Initiate* so you can stay aware of what is going on inside you.

❖ Actively manage your resistance instead of indulging in it or beating yourself up for feeling it.

❖ Make intentional, conscious choices about where you want to direct your energy and focus.

CREATE A MANTRA

Develop a personal mantra or saying for leading valiantly. Remember its essence and say it to yourself often. Here are some examples:

❖ "I am confident in my thoughts and actions."

❖ "I am willing to take action when I think it is right, even if it is not something I have done before and even if it is different from what others are doing."

❖ "I have a plan, and I am committed to seeing it through, even if I need to adjust it or accept a resolution that is 'good enough for now.'"

SURROUND YOURSELF WITH VALOR

Spend time with leaders you consider to be valiant. These can be individuals who think and do things the same way or differently from you. They can come from your discipline or different disciplines. They can be older or younger than you. No matter who they are, seek them out and watch and listen generously. Identify what it is about them that you consider to be valiant.

RECOGNIZING LEADERSHIP VALOR IN OTHERS

One way to deepen your appreciation of Leadership Valor and what practicing it can mean for you is to recognize it in others. When you spot a valiant leader, see if he or she has some of the characteristics Leah exhibits:

Leah is a leader who is comfortable with herself. She is clinically competent, and she is an exemplary leader who displays her mettle on regular occasions. Being in Leah's presence, even for a few hours, tells the story of how she affects others, creates extraordinary results, and manifests leading valiantly. These are just a few of the ways in which she does this:

❖ *Her vision is well-defined. She knows what she wants to achieve and when, and she knows what success looks like. She can describe all these things in some detail, and she also can leave the specifics behind to share her vision and inspire others.*

❖ *Leah is clear on whom she needs to bring on board to achieve these results, what resources they need to succeed, and how to help them be accountable to her and to themselves.*

❖ *She has a results-driven bias that is unwavering yet respected. She does not like excuses and tells her colleagues and direct reports exactly that. At the same time, she understands multiple priorities and human challenges and barriers.*

❖ *Leah consciously manages her own impact. She knows that others look up to her. She knows that what she says carries weight. She also knows that if she accepts humanity and humility in herself, she will model that for other people. So she does this by working 40–50 hours a week rather than the 60-plus hours that are standard elsewhere in the system.*

❖ *She never lets people forget why they are there.*

❖ *She generously acknowledges and celebrates success.*

Leah has done her own work on the journey of Leadership Valor. She admits that she can be captured by Seductions when she sees incompetence, especially when it is in her area or any area that will affect patient care. She acknowledges that she can be enticed by I Am Right, *and she practices letting it go. She much prefers using her expertise in ways that will support rather than hinder others' growth and success.*

Leah gives us an example of a leader who is "just doing her job." But in doing just what she was hired to do, she is leading valiantly every day. In "just" being a full version of who she is and achieving what she was hired to do, she is inspiring others to lead with their own versions of valor. Together, she and her team are on a quest to create sustainable and outstanding results for their patients and their community.

Consider whether you, too, have—or want to have—these characteristics. If you want to be more like Leah, what do you want to do more of, less of, or differently?

RECOGNIZING LEADERSHIP VALOR IN YOURSELF

As a truly valiant leader, you are the nurturer and the protector of your unique spirit and your deeply held values and beliefs. You are also a "content specialist" in yourself. You can be successful in these roles by intentionally cultivating and honing your self-awareness. You can do this by being an astute observer of how you are leading, what kind of impact you are having, and whether and how you want to supplement your efforts going forward.

Here are some of the qualities of valiant leadership you might see in yourself. As you read this list, think about how you would rate yourself on each of these characteristics. In what areas do you excel? Are there some you want to strengthen?

❖ You are clear. You know and claim who you are and what you stand for. You are aware of your heart as well as your mind.

❖ You are flexible and self-correcting. You have the ability to be responsive, and you believe you are able to stay fluid and truly present in most situations.

❖ You are curious, you observe yourself, and you continue to learn about who you are. You actively develop and manage your leadership assets and are not afraid to acknowledge (to yourself and perhaps to others) areas in which you are not strong.

❖ You are aware of how you feel in your own skin. If you do not feel relaxed, you reflect on what you can do, practice, or think about to become more at ease.

❖ You choose what you pay attention to, and you are thoughtful about the people and the environments with which you surround yourself.

❖ You leverage the strengths you have as a leader. Like Angela in Vignette 8, you consider the times when they are additive and helpful. You are not afraid to "use" yourself effectively. At the same time, you know that not all aspects of your skill and expertise are relevant in every situation.

❖ Your level of self-confidence is not excessive or diminished; it is appropriate. You convey that you value yourself.

❖ You are confident and wise enough to let go of focusing on yourself when it's the right choice; you are able to take in information and input without getting defensive.

❖ You think about the leadership successes you are most proud of, and you identify what you did in those situations. You consciously nurture and *Integrate* this level of understanding of yourself, and you address whether and how that knowledge can help you in the future.

❖ You possess a degree of humility that you believe is appropriate. In most instances, you can accurately assess the reach and the limit of your own knowledge and power.

❖ You communicate clearly. You notice your internal dialogue, and you reflect on whether it includes distortions, Seductions, or other messages that inappropriately empower or disempower you or others.

❖ When you have feelings such as fear or other emotions you think are negative, you are aware of them but know that you do not have to articulate, act on, or be enslaved by them.

❖ You are aware of and honor your professional, personal, and relational boundaries. You are able to distinguish and act on what is yours to own, and what is others' to own, whether it is concrete or emotional.

❖ You do not abandon yourself. You are aware of your positions, your values, and your needs and consciously choose when to adhere to them, even in adversity, and when to adjust them.

❖ You manage your own personal agenda and choose how you want it to influence you and others.

PART III
SUSTAINING
SUCCESS AS A
VALIANT LEADER

In Part I of this book, you were introduced to Leadership Valor
in its fullest expression. You experienced Caroline's unique way of
leading valiantly, and you saw how her journey reflected her bravery,
integrity, her deep sense of self, and her heartfelt wishes to serve
those around her. You also witnessed the unfolding of Jackie's story
as she addressed the real challenges of leading every day. You saw
her choose to expand her self-awareness, access the steps in the
Cycle of Leadership Valor, consider her Seductions, renew her way
of leading valiantly, and achieve success on her own terms.

In Part II, you saw other forms of Leadership Valor, including snapshots of healthcare and nurse leaders who navigated circumstances that are familiar to all of us. You reviewed the practices and choices that guided them, and you considered exercises and questions that will help you on your own journey.

In Part III of *Leading Valiantly in Healthcare*, we will build on your knowledge of the essence and spirit of this kind of leadership. In Chapter 5, we will review its less-obvious aspects so you can streamline and align it with your individual style.

Finally, in Chapter 6, we will examine what it means to master Leadership Valor. We will adjust the traditional models of mastery and move away from the pursuit of perfection. Instead, we will move toward the goal of leading valiantly on more occasions, more of the time. We will look at the powerful impact your mastery has on those around you. In the end, we will see how the ordinary becomes extraordinary as you incorporate valiant leadership into your work, your career, and your life.

5

How to Use the Cycle and the Steps of Leadership Valor

Embarking on the Cycle of Leadership Valor can enhance your self-awareness, the way you lead, and your ability to focus on others and yourself in your day-to-day life. Selecting one, a few, or all of the steps to reflect and act on can bring you into balance and integrity when you face a challenge. Whether you are ready, resistant, or both, Leadership Valor is available for you at any time.

So, too, are your options for how to manage the process, the mini-loop of expediency, the exercises, the steps, and the practices. The choices you make are likely to depend on:

❖ What is at stake

❖ How much you want to rely on your existing knowledge and expertise

❖ Your willingness to consider the Seductions

❖ Your readiness to shift your thinking and/or make adjustments in your behavior

❖ Your comfort with trying something new

Understanding the nuances of the journey to sustainable, valiant leadership is the focus of this chapter. Your familiarity with these subtleties will support you when you practice and shape Leadership Valor so it is uniquely your own.

Making the Process Yours

Remember that the Cycle and the steps are there to serve you as you claim and demonstrate the valor that is already within you. This section provides tips that will help you optimize the process.

The Need for Speed Does Not Apply

There is not an optimal speed for using the Cycle and the steps. For a significant journey of discovery, such as re-igniting dreams that you have long forgotten, engaging the process may take months or longer. But for others, this same transition could go much more quickly.

THE FOUR STEPS WORK FOR BIG DECISIONS—AND SMALLER ONES, TOO

The four steps can be used to clarify your thinking about all types of important, career-determining decisions, as well as those that are much less consequential. Jackie's use of the steps in Chapter 3 offers an example of how the steps can clarify routine choices that leaders commonly face on the job.

FOLLOWING ALL THE STEPS—ALL THE TIME—IS NOT REQUIRED

You won't want or need to follow all the steps every time you choose to lead valiantly. Once you are familiar with and have worked the Cycle several times, you can access a single step when you need it. For example, if you are about to make a harsh comment to a colleague, you can stop yourself by remembering that nurturing positive relationships is part of who you are at your core (an aspect of Step 2: *Illuminate*). Or, you may realize that you are about to be enticed into blaming someone else even though you are partially responsible for a situation (another aspect of *Illuminate*). In these and similar cases, you will decide how much or how little of the Cycle to engage at any given time.

"You won't want or need to follow all the steps every time you choose to lead valiantly."

There also may be times when you will do the work of one step, skip another, or come back later to one you already worked through. In this story, Stella offers us an example of skipping and returning to steps:

Stella is a strong leader, she is committed to leading with valor, she knows what is important to her at her core, and she is clear that she would like to have her boss's job when he retires in two years. At the moment, however, Stella has a habit of responding immediately when her boss wants something, even when it is on weekends or at unreasonable hours in the evening.

Stella has worked the steps, and she is satisfied that she revealed what she needs to know about her essence and aspirations in Illuminate. *This step gave her clarity on her short- and long-term goals and who she is at this point in her life. But in this situation, she repeatedly goes back to the rest of* Illuminate *(Recognizing Seductions) because she is prone to the sixth Seduction:* It's All About You. *Her version of this Seduction is that she focuses too much on what her boss wants instead of creating boundaries and standing up for herself to safeguard her own well-being.*

Stella has already chosen self-awareness and accessed her Three Levels of Reality, so she can skip *Initiate* and the first part of *Illuminate*. However, she needs to remind herself about the second part of *Illuminate* and the Seduction *It's All About You* until she breaks her habit of saying "yes" to her boss in every circumstance, regardless of time and place.

FEELINGS COUNT

Another nuance of leading with valor is how we feel about doing it. Most leaders face tough moments of decision, and possibly temporary indecision, on the job. At times, leaders have mixed feelings about making these difficult calls. And for some leaders, being conflicted is common.

In the world of valiant leadership, having mixed feelings is normal. Exemplary leaders can be clear about what is right to do given who they are at their core, their dreams, their clarity about Seductions, and their plans for moving forward. They can even identify with most or all of the indicators of readiness in Table 4.1 (see Chapter 4). But they can still be conflicted. For example, leaders may be committed to making budget reductions that will result in layoffs. No matter how committed they are to reducing costs, they may feel personally saddened because their decisions will significantly impact the lives of their colleagues and their families.

You, too, may feel conflicted when you lead valiantly. As we explored in Chapter 4, you may be both ready and resistant at the same time. Or, you may be ready and fearful. Let's say you are somewhat afraid of volunteering a point of view that you expect to be challenged by your co-workers. At the same time, you still feel it is the right thing to do. In this case, you can embrace your readiness and move ahead while also acknowledging your fears and being kind to yourself.

There is benefit to acknowledging rather than pushing aside multiple feelings, even when they conflict. In doing so, we allow ourselves the whole of our humanity. We give ourselves room to recommit or reconsider our plans and positions. We acknowledge that we are complex beings who may have more than one priority. For example, we may be committed to spending time with our families, and we may also be dedicated to our work. Acknowledging multiple feelings and competing concerns, rather than recognizing only one perspective, opens us to the rest of what is true. Pushing the rest aside may give us solace in the short run, but it will not allow us to feel whole, act with integrity, or serve others well in the long run.

"There is benefit to acknowledging rather than pushing aside multiple feelings, even when they conflict. In doing so, we allow ourselves the whole of our humanity."

In their seminal article in the *Harvard Business Review,* Robert Kegan and Lisa Lahey (2001) note the prevalence of competing commitments and their influence on leaders' capacities to change. Valiant leadership openly acknowledges more than one feeling or commitment precisely so you know what you are facing and understand how your thoughts and feelings align with or conflict with each another. As you move through the Cycle and cultivate your leadership, your plans will reflect a more complete, coherent strategy even if you are conflicted, or ready and resistant, at the same time.

STALLING AND GETTING STUCK ARE NORMAL—STAYING STUCK IS NOT

Sometimes we get stuck on the way to being valiant leaders. Stalling can happen at any point in the Cycle.

Leaders can get stuck before even reaching *Initiate* when they automatically move straight to resolution rather than choosing to step back and pause. Essentially, this means taking the mini-loop of expediency without thinking and for the wrong reasons. Because this is such a common habit for busy leaders, there's a section about this dynamic later in the chapter.

For now, here are a few examples of what stalling, getting stuck, and staying stuck in each of the steps look like.

Step 1: Initiate

Being excessively attached to the action of the mini-loop is common for many leaders, and for them, getting stuck in self-awareness is not usually a problem. However, there are leaders who have a natural affinity for reflection. These individuals benefit greatly from their thoughtful natures, but some may linger too long in contemplation. They may be doing this because they prefer quiet moments or because they are shying away from taking action, even after they have gained all the self-awareness they need. Either way, they are "stuck" in this first step, and they will benefit from giving themselves a gentle "push" to move on.

Step 2: Illuminate

Some leaders will get lost in questions of essence; after all, the matter of "Who am I?" has occupied philosophers for millennia. Along the way these leaders will get stuck in the muck of this or other potentially confounding questions. Or, as noted in Chapter 4, we can resist understanding more about ourselves: what is true at our core, what our dreams are now, and/or what our Seductions are. We might also think that this step simply requires too much heavy lifting, and when the answers to its questions are not right in front of us, we may grow frustrated.

If you are prone to deep and prolonged consideration of these important questions, it may help to look for answers that are "good enough" for now. You can always revisit your conclusions. Getting to a "good enough" resolution will allow you to move on, and achieving a "good enough" state can be consistent with being a valiant leader, as we explored in Chapter 3.

Step 3: Curate

There are times when we as leaders are not able to come up with a plan. Or, we may have a plan, get feedback, make a new plan, get more feedback, and change the plan again. And on and on. This process may not look like stalling and getting stuck because of all the action that seems to be taking place. But unless progress toward the goal is occurring, we are "busy" but we are not getting to resolution.

People often confuse perpetual discussion and planning with progress. We can see this in a common leadership complaint: their colleagues "recycle" the same issues again and again in meetings. It's easy to spot this tendency when we are the observers. We can use the same observational skill to catch ourselves when we are confusing continual planning with forward motion.

Step 4: Integrate

We may love learning and overstay our welcome in this step. Getting stuck here takes us too far out of the action of leadership and too far into thinking about leading rather than actually doing it. If this applies to you, consider whether there is action that you are avoiding by staying in the thinking mode instead. You may say no, but if you say yes, consider what you need to do to let go of so much focus on learning and integration so you can return to the "stage" of leading.

Another way of being stuck with *Integrate* is simply not to do it. Deliberate reflection and conscious learning may not have a place in your day, your week, or, eventually, your life. If you identify with this, consider whether you are stuck in a habit that prevents you from reaping the benefits of learning.

In short, it is normal and human to get stuck at any point as we move through the steps. If this happens to you, it's important to acknowledge the reasons for becoming entrenched and to let go of what brought you to a standstill.

Managing the Mini-Loop of Expediency

In Chapter 3, you read about the mini-loop of expediency (pictured again in Figure 5.1), and you saw it in action in some of the vignettes in Part II. So far, you've seen it as a closed loop that does not prompt more self-awareness or the choice of using the steps. As you will see in the following sections, there are times when choosing the mini-loop is appropriate, and other times when choosing it limits your potential for valiant leadership.

FIGURE 5.1   THE MINI-LOOP OF EXPEDIENCY

WHEN TO USE THE MINI-LOOP

When you first learned about the mini-loop in Chapter 3, it was presented as a default go-to strategy, a hard-wired reaction that did not serve Jackie. However, there are many circumstances in which using the mini-loop is the right choice. Here are some examples:

❖ You have the expertise you need to make a decision and act.

❖ The solution is straightforward, and you are ready to just "do it." Even if you do not have all the information you could use, you know enough.

❖ It is an emergency, and there is no time for gathering more information, reflecting on the facts, and involving others.

"There are times when choosing the mini-loop is appropriate, and other times when choosing it limits your potential for valiant leadership."

When Not to Use the Mini-Loop

We see in the preceding examples that there are many good reasons to simply resolve a situation when it appears. There are also less-than-valiant motives for moving quickly from a situation to a resolution, as the following two misguided uses of the mini-loop show.

You Think the Need for Speed Does Apply—All the Time

Some leaders won't choose the Cycle, even when it is fitting. That may be because they are biased toward action. Characters in film and television often depict an extreme version of this style when they embody a volatile and reactive form of leadership. While this may be entertaining on screen, it is a lot less appropriate as a customary way of making decisions in real life. Yet, more than a few organizations promote an "act now and act fast" approach to business, even the business of healthcare.

Just as some organizations and societies condone this leadership style, there are also some leaders who have personally adopted the "need for speed." This may be so ingrained in their DNA that solving problems right now has become both a positive and a negative characteristic. The upside is that these leaders are probably known for quick decisions and prompt results. The downside is that they may choose this strategy in every instance, even when it is ill-advised.

YOU, LEADING VALIANTLY

If acting quickly is your default *modus operandi* and you suspect you use it too often, notice the next time you are tempted to do this *even when it is not the best choice.*

❖ Ask yourself: What is my motivation for taking action now?

- Be honest with yourself and see if your answer is, essentially, that you would like to get to resolution so you can take this issue off your plate.

- Ask yourself if this is true even though you do not know enough about the facts, you may not have the best solution, and there is no harm in pausing.

❖ If you answered "yes" to these questions, see if you can resist the temptation to act. It might be uncomfortable, but think about whether you want to *Initiate* the Cycle instead.

- Consider whether you can avoid a bigger problem (as well as greater discomfort) in the future by getting more information or taking a more thoughtful approach right now.

- Think about whether there are times when initiating a more deliberate process of reflection will yield better outcomes than acting quickly.

Exclusive Use of the Mini-Loop Limits Learning

True experts know that there is never a point at which they have learned everything about their chosen field. Valiant leaders at all levels of expertise know this, too. Even in the rapid-fire world of moving from problem to solution to problem again, *Initiating* self-awareness or moving right into the fourth step of *Integrating* new learning will enrich our wisdom and capacity for sustained excellence and valiant leadership.

MANAGING THE SUBTLETIES OF THE INDIVIDUAL STEPS

So far in this chapter, we have looked at the whole experience of leading valiantly, as well as when choosing the mini-loop will and won't serve you. Now, we turn to managing the nuances of the individual steps so they will work optimally for you. For your reference, Figure 5.2 contains the Cycle of Leadership Valor as introduced in Chapter 3.

THE NUANCES OF STEP 1: *INITIATE*

Just electing to *Initiate* contrasts with the impulse to rely solely on your expertise, wisdom, and skill when you simply know what to do. Instead, by *Initiating*, you opt to step back, metaphorically, so you can shed more light on yourself or your opportunity or both. You choose self-awareness.

FIGURE 5.2   THE FOUR STEPS OF LEADERSHIP VALOR

But the subtlety of this step is that taking it does not mean you will take all the rest. Once you are familiar with the Cycle, you may elect to skip one or more steps after taking this first one.

"Once you are familiar with the Cycle, you may elect to skip one or more steps after taking the first one."

Here's an illustration of what skipping *Illuminate* looks like. To glean the most from this example, imagine that it is about you.

> *You are having difficulty communicating with your boss because she is distracted with personal issues. She keeps saying, "You're do-ing fine," and dismissing your concerns rather than listening to the vexing issues you have in your service area. You keep trying to talk with her anyway, both to hear her ideas and to cover yourself if something negative happens. Your approach is not working. You are clear about your core and your commitment to patient care, and your long-term aspirations for the well-being of your staff and your patients, but you also know that a Seduction is taking root. As your frustration mounts, you are at the edge of jumping into* I Am Right. *Even as you think about this Seduction, you are convinced that, in fact, you* are *right: She should get over her distraction and pay attention. But, you also know that approaching your boss with this edge will not get the results you want. You want to do some-thing different, but what?*

Notice that you, as a valiant leader, elected to *Initiate* (Step 1) by pausing and reflecting on your options and *Curate* (Step 3) by considering and creating a new approach. Once you've created and implemented your new plan, perhaps adjusted it, and the situation is sufficiently resolved, it is likely that you'll think about whether it worked, and if so, which parts were most successful. If some or all of your strategy was not successful, you'll consider what didn't work. You'll be embodying Step 4: *Integrate*.

Note, too, that you have not given time and attention to *Illuminate* because you are already grounded in your Three Levels of Reality (consensus, essence, and dreaming), and you can see the Seduction as it is forming.

THE NUANCES (AND THE TRAP) OF STEP 2: *ILLUMINATE*

You already know the benefits of *Illuminating* and embracing the whole of who you are, including whether any of the Seductions are relevant for you. Just one advantage is that you are more likely to lead with personal and professional integrity. Walt Whitman's (1999) famous quote, "We convince by our presence," says what we need to know about the value of this step. A leader with clarity is compelling, and a leader with valor radiates integrity that is unmistakable. And, because we are clear, we are able to focus more directly on the people and opportunities in front of us rather than on ourselves.

BEING VALIANT

"A leader with clarity is compelling, and a leader with valor radiates integrity that is unmistakable."

While we can see the advantages of *Illuminating,* there is also a trap.

The Trap of Illuminating

Most of us have a "go-to" or natural level of reality in which we usually dwell. Data-driven leaders may focus on consensus reality, while those who are visionaries may concentrate primarily on aspirations and dreaming. Some leaders may be heavily mission driven, so essence is their customary reality. Being more comfortable and aligned with one reality over others is a natural tendency. The Guidepost below will help you identify which Level of Reality you tend to favor and help you understand the potential costs of that preference.

YOU, LEADING VALIANTLY

Take some time to consider the following questions:

❖ What level of reality is most comfortable and familiar to you as a leader?

❖ Imagine the focus of your attention as a big expanse and think about how you allocate each of the Three Levels within it.

  • Do you give each level equal time?

  • If not, which reality claims most of your attention? Approximately what percentage of your time do you focus on that reality?

  • What about the other two realities? What percentage of your time do you spend on those?

❖ What are the implications of your answers? For example, if you say that you spend about 90% of your time focused on consensus reality, how does that impact what you think is important at work? What about your aspirations and your core? Are they alive and well?

❖ Is there a significant imbalance in the way you focus your time? And, if you lead others, how do you think this imbalance affects them?

"Most of us have a 'go-to' or natural level of reality in which we usually dwell."

Your natural affinity for one reality may skew your view of what is important. This tendency can influence your judgment as well as your communication with your peers and colleagues. Although one level of reality may be most comfortable to you, that does not mean that it should consistently be most important in the larger context of your role.

When you communicate primarily from a single perspective, you may be sending messages that short-change other organizational concerns that are significant, too. It is also possible that the focus of your communication is wholly predictable and, on occasion, ineffective because your message is always the same.

For example, if you are focused on the bottom line and productivity and you are known for leading your team in this way, your team may anticipate your high expectations, or your mounting frustration, regarding how much they are accomplishing. It's quite possible that both you and your team are already working hard to achieve results. But notice whether both you and they are also lacking inspiration and exhibiting signs of burnout. If so, it may be because an exclusive diet of any single perspective quickly loses its capacity to inspire. In this example, too many prompts for productivity, and too many days and nights of hard work without honoring any other point of view, can be both physically and spiritually draining.

An important benefit of the Three Levels of Reality is that you can use your enriched perspective to bring yourself and your team back into balance. If you are feeling overwhelmed by difficult demands (usually stemming from consensus reality), the questions in the Guidepost that follows can help you find greater equilibrium.

YOU, LEADING VALIANTLY

Take your time as you consider these questions about your impact and the whole of your well-being as a valiant leader:

❖ How often do you remember why you are doing your work, who you are at your core, and what you offer people when you are inspired and refreshed?

❖ Can you give yourself permission to take the actions that will re-balance and nourish you—not just the "you" that operates in consensus reality by producing results, but the rest of you as well? If you can, you are more likely to lead with clarity, integrity, and your unique brand of valor.

The Nuances of Illuminate

The second step in the Cycle of Leadership Valor has several subtleties.

You are in charge. Asking the questions "Who am I?" and "What do I want?" can take you into a deep and significant personal examination of these potentially profound questions. As noted earlier in this chapter, you can also get stuck in these explorations. Remember that you can make the work of this step as easy or as difficult as you like. You are in charge of this journey, so you don't need to make it more demanding than you want.

"You are in charge of this journey, so you don't need to make it more demanding than you want."

Whatever your choice, notice that your answers to the questions about all Three Levels of Reality can be layered. There may not be just one answer to "What do you most want?" Or, you may have many ways of describing who you are at your core, and they can all be accurate.

If delving into multifaceted questions about your life and your dreams serves you, you can explore them deeply in *Illuminate*. If you will be better served by asking and quickly answering the questions:

- ❖ "Who am I—now, in this moment?"

- ❖ "What do I want—now, in this moment?"

- ❖ "What is happening—now, in this moment?"

that should be your approach to this step. The key is to make the step your own. You can adjust it so it is just right for one situation, and you can adjust it again for another.

Check your story. As you have seen, *Illuminating* can prompt useful thinking about your Three Levels of Reality and the Seductions.

For example, when you describe "what is happening" (your view of consensus reality), consider whether or not a Seduction might be distorting your representation of that reality, or if you are telling one of the "Six Stories" outlined in Part II. Is it possible, for instance, that you are exaggerating or minimizing the facts? If you have a troubling situation on your hands, consider whether you are embellishing any elements of the story. If so, what is the benefit of doing that? If you are not sure if you are seeing a situation clearly, look at the "Catch Yourself in the Act" exercise in "Perspectives and Tips: Sustaining Valor in the Face of *Storytelling*" in Part II.

Thinking about your own stories and getting others' perspectives may prompt you to revise your view of consensus reality. As a valiant leader, this is a valuable exchange because your use of the steps has helped you to adjust your viewpoint and possibly your plan of action.

Address the most important Seduction, and you will impact the others, too. Leadership Seductions often appear in groups, as noted in Chapter 2 and in Part II, and when they do, there is almost always one that is primary. If you can determine which one is paramount and let it go, it is more likely that the others will recede or dissolve altogether.

In the following anecdote, Marta walks us through how she achieves success by disempowering her Seductions. She does this by identifying the "ring leader," changing her internal dialogue, and choosing to let her principal Seduction go.

Marta is about to step into a meeting with Ralph. Although he is not her boss, he holds a more senior position than she does, and she needs to work productively with him on a joint project. She is not looking forward to this meeting. Most of her interactions with him leave her feeling frustrated and angry. When she talks with others, she calls him a poor leader and an incompetent clinician.

What is different now is that Marta is doing her best to lead with valor, so she thinks about how she can make this meeting success-ful, not only for the organization, but also for herself and even for Ralph. First, she takes a look at the Seductions. When she is really honest with herself, she realizes that there are three Seductions that she needs to explore:

- ❖ *Seduction 1:* I Am Right

- ❖ *Seduction 2:* Storytelling

- ❖ *Seduction 6:* It's All About You

Although Marta is not pleased with this realization, she knows she has a new and significant level of self-awareness.

Next, she thinks about which of the Seductions is most important. She tests each one by asking herself if the others would be less influ-ential if she eliminated that particular one. It is easy for her to see the malleable nature of Storytelling. *She would be open to chang-ing her stories about this physician if either her righteous belief about herself (*I Am Right*) or her focus on him (*It's All About You*) were eliminated. This tells her that* Storytelling *is not her main Seduction.*

So she shifts her focus to I Am Right. *She really believes she is right, so she can't bring herself to eliminate that one. Finally, she turns her attention to* It's All About You. *In making that shift, she realizes that she has been completely convinced that it was all about Ralph. She has not considered what her part might be in their difficult interactions. As she thinks about this further, she decides to step away—at least momentarily—from her conviction that her difficulty with him is entirely his fault. She is willing to try to listen more openly to his ideas. She decides that if she can do this and produce a successful outcome, it is possible that she could let go of the stories she is telling and her total conviction that she is right. She is willing to give it a try.*

Significantly, Marta does not feel she has to let go of her judgment on the substance of the topics they were discussing. But she wants to give Ralph another chance by listening to him more openly than she has previously.

When you next encounter the Seductions and you start to feel their influence, remember Marta's experience. Think about her ability to identify the Seduction that was most compelling and more important than the others. By borrowing her technique, you may be able to defuse the Seductions more quickly than would be possible otherwise.

THE NUANCES OF STEP 3: *CURATE*

Curating your unique approach to Leadership Valor calls for stepping up, and it can take time to assume more responsibility in your role and lead in new and more courageous ways. Here is an example:

You are used to being a successful mid-level leader. You are competent in your own right, but you are used to operating with the guidance and support of others in the organization who are more influential than you are. This allows you to get a lot done and feel powerful, too. But you have recently done the work of the previous step (Illuminate), *and as a result, you are clear about what is truly important to you and how you want to manifest it in the world.*

Your newfound clarity and your commitment to lead with valor require you to lead differently. Eventually, they may prompt you to take a different job, one that gives you more direct line responsibility and one that takes you out of the shadow of other leaders. The changes you want to make will likely not happen overnight. Instead, it is probable that you will need to "try on" and practice this new version of yourself for at least some period of time before you are ready to seek another position. When you do look for another job, you will want to be thoughtful about the post you select and its potential to provide the career boost you seek.

Calibrating (part of Step 3: *Curate)* consciously and deliberately is a learned skill. Here are two dynamics you will want to consider as you take this step.

"Check the Fit" of Feedback

As a valiant leader, it is likely that you will become more aware of feedback and how you receive it. You owe yourself the chance to evaluate input in skillful ways. One element of this skill is to "check the fit" of critical comments that are made about you or to you. Checking the fit means considering whether the feedback is reasonable. If the feedback is negative, does some, but not all, of the criticism ring true? Calibrating gives you the chance to thoughtfully consider others' input, and whether and how you want to adjust your responses and your actions going forward. Sometimes you will want to modify your strategy, and at other times you will reaffirm it, even if others object.

Through practice, you can also learn how to skillfully communicate when feedback suggests that you change what you are doing. Telling others you are changing your mind is complicated territory for you and every leader, as popular political discourse shows. However, as a leader who leans into leading valiantly, practice will prepare you and you will be up to the task.

Be Aware of Consequences

As noted in Chapter 4, calibration also allows for making mistakes and owning them when they occur. How you demonstrate accountability for errors in judgment is up to you. But when you do assume responsibility for errors you have made, one of the reactions is likely to be that other people will respect your honesty. There may be other consequences, to be sure, but at least you will have the opportunity to act with integrity. And valor.

THE NUANCES OF STEP 4: *INTEGRATE*

As noted earlier in this chapter, the biggest nuance of *Integrating* is the great temptation not to take the step at all. While no amount of rhetoric can convince busy leaders to stop and take in what they are learning, it is worth considering the value that *Integrating* can offer you, just as it offered Roger in Vignette 10. Here are a few perspectives that can help you take this step more often:

❖ The next time a situation or tough challenge presents itself, you will have more wisdom and skill to draw upon. It is also likely that you will have more confidence because you have thought about what you have done well and not so well in similar circumstances.

❖ *Integrating* can be time-consuming, but it does not have to be. How much time does it take to think about an interaction you just had and whether it went well? How much time does it take to check in with how you feel about your way of leading and the results you are producing?

As noted earlier in this chapter, you can leave out one or more steps as you become familiar with them. Ironically, the one step you may not want to eliminate in any instance is this one. You can learn in nearly every interaction in which your resolve is tested or an opportunity is taken. Choosing to *Integrate* what you have learned will reward you every time.

BEING VALIANT

"You can learn in nearly every interaction in which your resolve is tested or an opportunity is taken."

Integrating will become almost automatic as you learn the art of leading with valor. In fact, in my experience, leaders who learn when to take the mini-loop, skip steps, and navigate their nuances are well on their way to mastering valiant leadership, the subject of the next chapter.

KEY TAKE-AWAYS

❖ The steps can be used to clarify your thinking about important, career-determining decisions, as well as those that are much less consequential. For a significant journey of discovery, engaging the process can take months or longer. For less-profound situations, you can move through the steps much more quickly.

❖ You do not need to follow all the steps every time you choose to lead valiantly. Once you are familiar with and have worked the Cycle a few times, you may want to access only one or two steps when an opportunity or challenge arises.

❖ You can get stuck at any point in the Cycle. Stalling and getting stuck are normal. Staying stuck is not. Understanding the traps and nuances of each step will increase your skill and give you greater access to valiant leadership.

❖ There are many circumstances in which using the mini-loop is the right choice. There are also instances in which using the mini-loop does not serve you as a valiant leader.

❖ When Leadership Seductions appear in groups, there is almost always one that is "primary." If you can determine which one is paramount and let it go, it is likely that the others will recede or dissolve altogether.

6

MASTERING
VALIANT
LEADERSHIP

This book is an invitation. You have walked the full path of leading with valor and considered its unique expressions throughout this book. Now it's your turn to put its lessons to work for you. But how do you do that in a practical and realistic way? How can you incorporate a renewed and fortified leadership strategy into what you do every day without adding another task to your already overflowing plate? That's what we will explore in this final chapter. First, let's consider what might be your ultimate goal for leading with full integrity, bravery, and valor: mastery.

"How can you incorporate a renewed and fortified leadership strategy into what you do every day without adding another task to your already overflowing plate?"

MASTERY DEFINED

In healthcare the word *mastery* is often coupled with being an expert. In fact, you may be reminded of the novice-to-expert continuum and Patricia Benner's work referenced in Chapter 4. This model, so widely used as a way of understanding skill development in nursing, is an appropriate place to begin our exploration of mastery and valiant leadership.

THE NOVICE-TO-EXPERT CONTINUUM

We know from the seminal work of Patricia Benner (1984)—and before her the work of Stuart Dreyfus (1981) and Stuart and Hubert Dreyfus (1984)—that there is a logical progression of skill and competency acquisition. In *Novice to Expert: The Dreyfus Model of Skill Acquisition*, Stan Lester (2005) summarizes the Dreyfus brothers' research findings. Learners move through levels of skill attainment starting with the novice stage and concluding with the expert stage. As noted in the chart that appears in the Appendix:

❖ "Novices" are beginners who need rules and guidelines when they are starting to acquire a new skill. As learners become more adept, they progress through stages that eventually free them from following "recipes."

❖ Eventually, when they move through the stages of "advanced beginner" and "competent," they become "proficient." This is the point at which they approach situations more "holistically." They can see what is most important, and they make decisions accordingly.

❖ When they reach the "expert" stage, they have integrated the rules to such an extent that they can follow or deviate from them with ease. As the Dreyfus brothers note, experts allow their intuition to guide them, they possess vision for what is possible, and they can easily move between intuitive and analytical approaches when novel situations and problems appear.

The progressive acquisition of skill that appears in both Benner's work and the Dreyfuses' models is based in part on the essential notion of practice. None of us is surprised by the importance of repetition, but that importance gained traction with Malcolm Gladwell's best-selling book *Outliers*. He notes that a key to mastery of any endeavor is practice: lots and lots of practice. In fact, Gladwell (2008) defines the amount of practice needed for "success" as 10,000 hours. That's about 20 hours a week for 10 years!

MASTERY, PRACTICE, AND LEADERSHIP VALOR

So, if you want to lead valiantly with more intention than before, where do you start? Are you a novice or an expert, or are you somewhere in between? Do you need to practice for 10,000 hours to master valiant leadership?

Only you can answer that question, but it's doubtful that you will require that much practice. That's because mastering valiant leadership invites you to develop and practice leading this way more and more of the time, as opposed to 100% of the time. Wonderful as it would be to lead valiantly in every interaction, for most of us, that is an unattainable goal. In contrast, reaching a state of full-out courageous leadership *more often* is possible. The more you practice, the more you will have the experience of valiant leadership captured in Part II's "Perspectives and Tips: Recognizing Leadership Valor in Yourself." How much you choose to practice is entirely your call.

Whether you choose to rehearse a little or a lot, you'll want to consider these points:

❖ Practicing Leadership Valor is both a destination and a process. The act of rehearsing will enrich your learning at every step. Practice will further your journey toward being a master of valiant leadership, and it will expand your self-awareness along the way.

❖ If you have been in a stewardship role for any period of time, it is likely you are already leading with valor, at least occasionally, if not frequently. While this book and its steps and nuances may be conceptually new to you, the need for bold leadership, even when it is difficult, is not. No matter where you would place yourself on the novice-to-expert continuum, the invitation offered by this book is to lead this way consciously and more often, in ways that work for you. Practice will help you achieve that goal.

❖ If you and others acknowledge your expertise in clinical or other arenas, claim that knowledge with the dignity you have earned. But also note that the pursuit of Leadership Valor is different. This quest invites you to reflect on and practice only one facet of your expertise: your prowess as a valiant leader. Very few of us are experts in every aspect of our work, so if this is an area you can strengthen, know that you are in good company.

❖ Achieving an expert level of leading valiantly will not mean that you are challenge-free. Indeed, the number and quality of your challenges (and opportunities) may be wholly independent of your skill. In fact, you may return to the same issues again and again. For example, if you are particularly prone to Seduction 1: *I Am Right*, you could be playing out a lifelong preference for control. It is unrealistic to think that you will quickly rid yourself of this deeply ingrained habit, even when you are an expert at valiant leadership. However, it is likely that each time you discover, once again, that Seduction has you in its clutches, you will bring more wisdom to the current situation, and you will spot the Seduction faster.

As you practice, you will become more at ease with leading valiantly. You will determine when to follow all the steps, some of the steps, and/or when to go back to a step to take a second look.

Whether you consider yourself a beginner starting with *Initiate* and finishing with *Integrate*, or you are already using the steps in your own way, you are on the way to mastering Leadership Valor. Even if you are an intuitive expert at valiant leadership, you may want to try following the steps as they are arranged, at least at the beginning. You can improve how you lead by deliberately answering the questions in each step and thoughtfully integrating the wisdom that your answers contain.

MASTERY STARTED AND MASTERY SUSTAINED

No matter where you are on the novice-to-expert continuum, you can practice in any situation that offers you an occasion to lead in brave, powerful, and robust ways. Remember that the opportunities to lead with valor do not have to be grand in scale. They can be simply the stuff of every day leadership.

Just the act of reading this book acquaints you with Leadership Valor, and making this investment means that you are more likely to practice it. Your experience of revitalized leadership may be infrequent at first, but with more awareness and practice, you will find yourself leading valiantly more often.

"Remember that the opportunities to lead with valor do not have to be grand in scale."

Sustaining yourself as a valiant leader has similarities with sustaining yourself as a leader of any kind. You know the adages about caring for self. You probably also know how hard it is to truly care for yourself in a world of frequent interruptions, multiple priorities, and heavy demands.

Some leaders are not in a position to create and practice a real self-care regimen. The practice of leading with valor does not insist on self-care, so whether you embrace, practice, or even resist self-care is entirely your choice. That said, do note that the capacity for sustained success with this and any robust form of leadership is most rewarding when you nourish yourself.

As you become accustomed to leading more courageously, the results you achieve and the learning you take in will create their own momentum. Your experience of success and calibration will prompt you to practice more, to learn more, and to achieve more. You may also grow accustomed to leading bravely, even if you are afraid. Living with valor and occasional fear may begin to feel normal as you do it more frequently, and you may begin to experience valor as Michel de Montaigne described it: "Valor is stability, not of legs and arms, but of courage and the soul" (de Montaigne, 2009, p. 148).

Mastery and Others

Your work with Leadership Valor will have an impact on those around you. With thought and intention, you can understand and manage that impact so it helps others grow and sustains you as well. As you master valiant leadership, here are some of the ways in which you can relate to your co-workers with increased awareness and skill.

YOU WILL BE MORE PRESENT FOR OTHERS.

To lead with valor is to make conscious choices. You can choose to focus on yourself until you are clear about your positions and aspirations in given leadership situations. As you go back "out" to the circumstantial challenges of your role, you will know yourself well enough to hold your center more frequently. You will have the confidence to let go of your inward focus and shift your attention to other people.

"You will have the confidence to let go of your inward focus and shift your attention to other people."

This may contrast with challenges in which you are less clear about yourself and what you want to do. When you have less clarity, you may conflate your own needs with others' needs and demands because you have not addressed what's happening for you. This blurring of the boundaries between what is true for you and what is true for them can mean you are less present for them and the situation. That's because you are more occupied with personal concerns that you have not fully addressed and understood.

But by engaging with the Cycle, you will be better able to meet your colleagues where they are. Subtle as this sounds, a shift in your ability to be present with others can lead to profound differences in your relationships. How often does the press of business call for us to simply rush in with our agenda and our way of doing things, even if neither takes account of what is happening for other people? ("Other people" can be direct reports, peers, or even bosses with whom we only have a few minutes.) In the absence of an authentic connection with ourselves, we can simply gloss over what's happening with those around us. Worse, we can project our own moods onto them and misinterpret their reactions. Such bumpy interactions can cause us to decouple from not only the circumstances but also the people with whom we are working.

YOU WILL RELATE AND LISTEN DIFFERENTLY.

Your clarity about your aspirations, your essence, and your plan will give you direction. The option to calibrate will give you choice in whether and how you want to shift your trajectory if you encounter objections or receive new information.

Your familiarity with the Seductions will shed light on barriers that may be influencing you; that familiarity will also inform you about potential Seductions that may be at play for others, too. Your speculation about their Seductions can be an asset for you, but it can also backfire. The backfire can occur if you decide that you "know" what their Seductions are, and then you tell them about it. Notice that your diagnosis of another's Seductions may be your own Seductions in disguise.

Your suspicions about another's Seductions can be an asset only if you bring *all* your knowledge of the Seductions to bear. This means realizing that your ideas about their Seductions are not actual diagnoses; they are only hunches. Even if they are accurate, you know from your own experience how important it is for you, and not someone else, to identify your Seductions. This is not just true for you; it is true for everyone else, too. You also know that only you can decide if and when you will let a Seduction go. This, too, is true for everyone else.

What's important is to allow others the same freedom you give yourself when it comes to identifying and dealing with Seductions. When you do that, bringing your knowledge of the Seductions to your relationships will create more authentic connections along with greater mutual understanding and empathy.

YOU CAN SEE OTHERS MORE HUMANELY.

This journey of Leadership Valor introduces you to your own humanity over and over again. You will become familiar with checking in with yourself in deep, small, or in-between ways so you can embrace your integrity and lead with your full measure of power. This is true for those around you, too. As Stephen Covey (2008) says, "We tend to judge others based on their behavior, and ourselves based on our intent" (p. 84). Embracing Leadership Valor will provide you more wisdom, and perhaps you will judge others not just by their behavior, but by their intentions, too.

In other words, we may see people who work with and for us with more empathy because we can accept their humanity as well as our own. Seeing others this way also applies to how we see leaders we greatly admire. It is tempting to idealize exceptional leaders. We want them to be no less than excellent in every way, all the time. But perhaps we can give those we most admire a break and allow them to be human, too.

YOU MAY CHOOSE TO INVITE COLLEAGUES ON THE JOURNEY.

There are many ways to involve your co-workers so they, too, can grow as valiant leaders. You may also wish to enlist their support as you practice new skills and propose revised approaches to your shared problems. The myriad ways in which others can participate in the journey can start with sharing stories and practices of Leadership Valor. Doing so will give you common language and generate collective insights because, at least at some level, you'll all be in this together.

Telling others about your experiences of leading valiantly can be helpful for you as well as instructional—and perhaps even motivational for them. With trusted others, sharing your Seductions and inviting them to tell you about theirs can be mutually enlightening. The key word here is *trusted*. Heavy as some of our Seductions can be, sharing them with those we value can make these attachments feel a little lighter or perhaps even lift them altogether. At the very least, you will know that others are on the journey, too, and you can offer each other support along the way.

YOU WILL INSPIRE OTHERS.

When you lead with valor, you will serve as an inspirational leader for those around you. You may want to help them as they go on their own journeys; there are many ways for you to do that. One thing is certain: Your impact will stem from your own authentic practice of leading valiantly. What you *do* will be far more powerful than what you *say*. As you transform yourself, you invite others to do the same.

> *"As you transform yourself, you invite others to do the same."*

LIVED MASTERY: THE ORDINARY BECOMES EXTRAORDINARY

This is the point on this journey when we leave details behind and return to the essence of Leadership Valor. The nuances of learning the skill are important to understand as you customize and assimilate the process so it is yours. Still, the sum of the specifics is not the whole of valiant leadership. Much as you might like to capture the entirety of your rich, compelling, and valiant way of leading in an easy, step-wise process, you cannot. Rather, you can understand the steps and their subtleties, add them to your array of leadership practices, and use them to improve what you do. As you do, sooner or later, you will master the "state" of Leadership Valor.

The experience of leading with valor can create a deep and abiding sense of well-being. This is a way of leading that releases the best in you. It holds and channels your focus, your motivation, and your connection with yourself and others. Mihaly Csikszentmihalyi (1990) called this "flow" in his book *Flow: The Psychology of Optimal Experience*.

The notion of optimal experience or skill is valuable in many contexts, yet here we want to adjust the idea of "optimal" because it suggests an unattainable state of perfect leadership. Rather than mythologizing the mastery of Leadership Valor as "peak" performance, you will simply start to feel a new sense of personal power. You will believe in yourself more as you lead more bravely and in a manner that draws fully on who you are and what you want to achieve.

And, at some point, you will have practiced, refined, and integrated the learning from your practice in ways that are entirely natural for you. There will be occasions when you can whole-heartedly embrace the power—and the results—of leading valiantly. There will be other times when you won't do it perfectly, and that's part of this journey, too. Progress is the process and the outcome of mastering valiant leadership; perfection is not.

At that juncture, you will be leading like the leader you want to be, more and more of the time. You, and only you, will define when the moment arrives. That's when you will say you have stepped into a place of deep integrity, and you will fully and completely claim your unique form of valiant leadership.

NOVICE TO EXPERT: THE DREYFUS MODEL OF SKILL ACQUISITION

The material in this appendix is reprinted with permission from Stan Lester.

Introduction

This document contains two versions of the Dreyfus 'novice to expert' model, one combining the main features of both versions of the model published in the early 1980s, and the other taken from the institute of Conservation's professional standards.

The Dreyfus model is used fairly widely (a) to provide a means of assessing and supporting progress in the development of skills or competencies, and (b) to provide a definition of acceptable level for the assessment of competence or capability

The 'expert' level does not signify that development stops, as expert practitioners need to evaluate their practice and keep up-to-date with new evidence.

Introduction and adaptations of the Dreyfus model by Stan Lester.

Further Reading

Dreyfus, H L and Dreyfus, SE (1986). *Mind over Machine: the power of human intuition and expertise in the age of the computer.* Oxford, Basil Blackwell

Benner, P (1984). *From novice to expert: excellence and power in clinical nursing practice.* Menlo Park CA, Addison-Wesley

APPENDIX

Novice-to-Expert scale (1)

Level	Stage	Characteristics	How knowledge etc is treated	Recognition of relevance	How context is assessed	Decision-making
1	Novice	Rigid adherence to taught rules or plans Little situational perception No discretionary judgement	Without reference to context	None	Analytically	Rational
2	Advanced beginner	Guidelines for action based on attributes or aspects (aspects are global characteristics of situations recognisable only after some prior experience) Situational perception still limited All attributes and aspects are treated separately and given equal importance				
3	Competent	Coping with crowdedness Now sees actions at least partially in terms of longer-term goals Conscious, deliberate planning Standardised and routinised procedures	In context	Present		
4	Proficient	Sees situations holistically rather than in terms of aspects Sees what is most important in a situation Perceives deviations from the normal pattern Decision-making less laboured Uses maxims for guidance, whose meanings vary according to the situation			Holistically	Intuitive
5	Expert	No longer relies on rules, guidelines or maxims Intuitive grasp of situations based on deep tacit understanding Analytic approaches used only in novel situations or when problems occur Vision of what is possible				

Adapted from: Dreyfus, S E (1981) *Four models v human situational understanding: inherent limitations on the modelling of business expertise* USAF Office of Scientific Research, ref F49620-79-C-0063; Dreyfus, H L & Dreyfus, S E (1984) "Putting computers in their proper place: analysis versus intuition in the classroom," in D Sloan (ed) *The computer in education: a critical perspective* Columbia NY, Teachers' College Press.

Novice-to-Expert scale (2)

	Knowledge	Standard of work	Autonomy	Coping with complexity	Perception of context
1. Novice	Minimal, or 'textbook' knowledge without connecting it to practice	Unlikely to be satisfactory unless closely supervised	Needs close supervision or instruction	Little or no conception of dealing with complexity	Tends to see actions in isolation
2. Beginner	Working knowledge of key aspects of practice	Straightforward tasks likely to be completed to an acceptable standard	Able to achieve some steps using own judgement, but supervision needed for overall task	Appreciates complex situations but only able to achieve partial resolution	Sees actions as a series of steps
3. Competent	Good working and background knowledge of area of practice	Fit for purpose, though may lack refinement	Able to achieve most tasks using own judgement	Copes with complex situations through deliberate analysis and planning	Sees actions at least partly in terms of longer-term goals
4. Proficient	Depth of understanding of discipline and area of practice	Fully acceptable standard achieved routinely	Able to take full responsibility for own work (and that of others where applicable)	Deals with complex situations holistically, decision-making more confident	Sees overall 'picture' and how individual actions fit within it
5. Expert	Authoritative knowledge of discipline and deep tacit understanding across area of practice	Excellence achieved with relative ease	Able to take responsibility for going beyond existing standards and creating own interpretations	Holistic grasp of complex situations, moves between intuitive and analytical approaches with ease	Sees overall 'picture' and alternative approaches; vision of what may be possible

From the professional standards for conservation, Institute of Conservation (London) 2003 based on the Dreyfus model of skill acquisition.

REFERENCES

Benner, P. (1984). *From novice to expert: Excellence and power in clinical nursing practice.* Menlo Park, CA: Addison-Wesley.

Brown, E. (2009). Plato's ethics and politics in *The Republic.* In E. N. Zalta (Ed.), *The Stanford encyclopedia of philosophy* (Winter 2011 ed.). Retrieved from http://plato.stanford.edu/archives/win2011/entries/plato-ethics-politics/

Carlisle, C. (2003). Nietzsche's beyond good and evil: 'Why insist on truth?' *Richmond Journal of Philosophy, 4*(2003 Summer), 1-7.

Covey, S. R. (2008). *The SPEED of trust: The one thing that changes everything.* New York, NY: Free Press.

Csikszentmihalyi, M. (1990). *Flow: The psychology of optimal experience.* New York, NY: Harper & Row.

Custodian [Def. 2]. (n.d.). In *Collins English Dictionary, Complete & Unabridged 10th Edition.* Retrieved from http://dictionary.reference.com/browse/custodian

de Mille, A. (1991). *Martha: The life and work of Martha Graham.* New York, NY: Random House.

de Montaigne, M. (2009). *The complete essays of Michel de Montaigne* (C. Cotton, Trans.). In W. C. Hazlitt (Ed.). Retrieved from http://www.digireads.com/Search.aspx?query=The+Complete+Essays+of+Michel+de+Montaigne

Dreyfus, H. L., & Dreyfus, S. E. (1984). Putting computers in their proper place: Analysis versus intuition in the classroom. In D. Sloan (Ed.), *The computer in education: A critical perspective.* New York, NY: Columbia Teachers College Press.

Dreyfus, S. E. (1981). *Formal models vs. human situational understanding: Inherent limitations on the modeling of business expertise.* USAF Office of Scientific Research, ref F49620-79-C-0063.

Ericsson, A. K., Prietula, M. J., & Cokley, E. T. (2007 Jul-Aug). The making of an expert. *Harvard Business Review, 85*(7/8), 114-121.

Fuller, F., & Fridjhon, M. (2007). Appendix B: Coaching the team, the organization, or the relationship. In *Co-active coaching: New skills for coaching people toward success in work and life* (pp. 285-286). Mountain View, CA: Davies-Black Publishing.

Gelb, M. (2000). *How to think like Leonardo Da Vinci: Seven steps to genius every day.* New York, NY: Random House Publishing Group.

Gladwell, M. (2008). *Outliers.* New York, NY: Little, Brown and Company.

Goldsmith, M. (2007). *What got you here won't get you there: How successful people become even more successful.* New York, NY: Hyperion.

Heifetz, R. A., & Linsky, M. (2002). *Leadership on the line: Staying alive through the dangers of leading.* Boston, MA: Harvard Business School Publishing.

Jones, D. (Producer). (1999). *Everyday Creativity* [Motion picture]. United States: Star Thrower Distribution, Inc.

Katie, B. (2002). *Loving what is: Four questions that can change your life.* New York, NY: Three Rivers Press.

Kegan, R., & Lahey, L. L. (2001 Nov.). The real reason people won't change. *Harvard Business Review, 79*(10), 85-92.

Lester, S. (2005). Novice to expert: The Dreyfus model of skill acquisition. Retrieved from http://www.sld.demon.co.uk/dreyfus.pdf

Maurer, R. (2009). Resistance to change—Why it matters and what to do about it. Retrieved from http://www.rickmaurer.com/wp/articles-and-white-papers/resistance-to-change-why-it-matters-and-what-to-do-about-it

Mindell, A. [Arnold], & Mindell, A. [Amy]. (2012). A few process work details. Retrieved from http://www.aamindell.net/category/processwork-theory-applications/what-is-processwork

Petrie, N. (2011). *Future trends in leadership development* [White paper]. Retrieved from http://www.ccl.org/leadership/pdf/research/futureTrends.pdf

Ready [Def. 4]. (n.d.). In *Merriam-Webster online dictionary* (11th ed.). Retrieved from http://www.merriam-webster.com/dictionary/ready

Robertson, J. (n.d.). Accurate. In *Robertson's words for a modern age: A dictionary of English vocabulary words derived primarily from Latin and Greek word families, presented individually and in family units, plus vocabulary quizzes.* Retrieved from http://wordinfo.info/

REFERENCES

Robinson-Walker, C. (1999). *Women and leadership in healthcare: The journey to authenticity and power.* San Francisco, CA: Jossey-Bass.

Tian, X., & Wang, T. Y. (2011). Tolerance for failure and corporate innovation. *Review of Financial Studies.* Retrieved from http://ssrn.com/abstract=1399707

Whitman, W. (1999). *Walt Whitman: Selected poems: 1855-1892: A new edition.* G. Schmigdall (Ed.). New York, NY: St. Martin's Press.

Whyte, D. (2002). *The heart aroused.* New York, NY: Doubleday.

INDEX